Sussex Re

Alexandra Ayton

To my husband Rupert for all his love and support

Published by Pomegranate Press,
Dolphin House, 51 St Nicholas Lane, Lewes, Sussex BN7 2JZ
pomegranatepress@aol.com
www.pomegranate-press.co.uk

ISBN: 978–1–907242–11–3

British Library Cataloguing-in-Publication Data.
A catalogue record for this book is available from the British Library

Printed and bound by 4edge Limited, 7A Eldon Way, Hockley, Essex SS5 4AD

Foreword

I first met Alexandra Ayton in February 2006, when I was editor of *South Downs Living*, a new lifestyle magazine in the BN6 area. Alexandra would spend hours researching and writing about our local history. Although her articles were only around a thousand words long, she would pack them full of interesting information and they were a joy to read.

Needless to say, many of our readers would turn straight to Alexandra's articles. Her book is full of wonderful information about famous events and people, ideal to pick up and read whenever you have some free time. However, be warned – it's so fascinating that you won't be able to put it down!

Connie Booth

Chesterton's in Ditchling was renamed after the famous writer. (Page 53)

The track of Volk's Electric Railway snaking below Madeira Drive.
(Page 63.)

Contents

The windmill at Rottingdean, well known to Rudyard Kipling (page 57) and Enid Bagnold (page 71).

Introduction

This book presents the stories of the many people and places that have shaped Sussex in the 19th and 20th centuries. Each essay has little known human-interest pieces and images to accompany it.

Read about landmarks such as the Balcombe Viaduct and the men who made it possible – the navvies; Devil's Dyke, as popular with Victorians and visiting royalty as it is today; the Egyptian pyramid in a small country churchyard; Lancing College Chapel, the fourth tallest ecclesiastical building in the country and much more.

The 19th century was a time when plants were being discovered, countries explored, education expanded and follies built to provide work for the local people. It was also a time when slavery was still 'acceptable' and divorce was a scandal on a grand scale.

The early 20th century heralded more changes: the dwindling empire, the devastation of World War One, the Indian warriors who were treated by Dr Brighton and those less fortunate who gave their lives for King George V, the King Emperor. It was a new day and age when Brighton's population and boundaries were expanding and inventors, writers and politicians were making a big impact.

More recently, the county has produced Grey Owl, a 'red Indian' from Hastings; Dame Grace Kimmins with her revolutionary approach to health care based on fresh air and sunshine; Henry Longhurst, the famous golf writer reluctantly sharing his home with a ghost; Sir Norman Hartnell, the world-famous royal dress designer; and, last but not least, the Brighton Belle, a train synonymous with elegance and comfort from a bygone era.

These twenty-five entertaining and varied sketches provide a wealth of information about notable people and events that have made Sussex what it is today.

Alexandra Ayton

Above: The Prayer Stone at Devil's Dyke.

Facing page: The stone in close-up.

The Legend and History of Devil's Dyke

Devil's Dyke boasts not only spectacular views in all directions but myths and legends that fascinate us as much today as our ancestors long ago.

It is the longest, deepest and widest dry chalkland valley in Britain with a very special name – 'Devil's Dyke' – which originates from the belief that the land was shaped by a supernatural force of some kind.

Some believe the Devil dug a tunnel on his way to the sea, others that the Devil was being chased away. One of the most famous legends turned into a comic strip by Geo Parkin is that of Saint Cuthman of Steyning travelling across the Sussex Weald to see Sister Ursula in Saddlescombe Chapel. Whilst admiring the many churches on route, Saint Cuthman encountered the Devil who threatened to wash away all the new churches by cutting a dyke through the hill to the sea that night.

Quick-thinking Saint Cuthman struck a bargain. If the Devil failed to complete his task by sunrise, he would leave them in peace! The saint told Sister Ursula and together they devised a plan. She would mark time with her hourglass and pray that with each hour the devil would tire and be unable to complete his wicked work! Meanwhile, Satan began digging a dyke from Chanctonbury Ring, Cissbury Ring, and Mount Caburn through to Firle Beacon.

The Devil became increasingly weary, and when dawn broke he had not completed his task. Humiliated, he retreated, leaving the inhabitants to live in peace on the unfinished dyke, which remains a symbol of good overcoming evil to this day.

Strange supernatural forces aside, the V-shaped valley was formed by the waters of the receding ice at the end of the last ice age and not by glacial action, another common misconception.

The summit offers spectacular views across the Weald and the South Downs. Further afield can be seen parts of Hampshire and Surrey including Botley Hill 29 miles away, and on a clear day, the Isle of Wight.

Archaeologically and ecologically diverse, Devil's Dyke is an environmentally sensitive area (ESA) and home to a variety of flora and fauna. Since 1995, the National Trust has managed Devil's Dyke Estate, which consists of Devil's Dyke, Wolstonbury Hill, Saddlescombe Farm, Newtimber Hill, Fulking Escarpment and Southwick.

Plants such as Lady's Bedstraw, Ribwort Plantain, Round-Headed Rampion and a variety of orchids thrive on the chalk grassland. Butterflies such as Grayling, Brown Argus, Adonis and Chalkhill Blues as well as the Emperor Moth, Small Elephant Hawk Moth and Orange Tailed Clearwing can be seen in season.

The Royal Seat at Devil's Dyke.

Historians can see the remains of a Norman motte and bailey castle, Bronze Age burial mounds and the hill fort ramparts, which reveal over 2000 years of life at the Dyke. For Victorians from the 1880s, Devil's Dyke was a tourist attraction with a fairground, swings, a spiral slide and a number of transport infrastructures.

Ernest Ryman's book, *Devil's Dyke in Old Picture Postcards*, describes how the Brighton-Dyke Railway ran from 1887 until 31st December 1938 with the exception of three years during World War I, when it ceased operating for economic reasons. Using mainly steam locomotives, the route was 5½ miles long from Brighton with 3½ miles of rising single track from the junction west of Hove known as Dyke Halt Junction until it was renamed Aldrington in 1932.

For its last journey in 1938, fog signals were fired, a band played and a crowd gathered to cheer nearly 400 passengers on board the 'Express'.

From 1894–1909, a cable car operated across Dyke Valley covering a distance of 350m hanging 70m above the ground where the four passengers delighted in dropping a piece of chalk from the cable car into the fields below. Nearly a hundred years later, all that remains are the rough concrete bases used to support the pylons forming part of the cable car system.

From 1897–1907 there was a 'Steep Grade Railway', a funicular rising 100m from near Poynings to the northern edge of the hill fort. Mr Hubbard, the landlord of the Dyke Hotel in Dyke Park installed two bandstands, an observatory and a model of a 110-ton cannon. There was also a coffee room for up to 275 people where tea and bread and buttercake or soda and milk were available.

Buses were a great joy. In May 1893, the *Devil's Dyke Times* wrote: 'The road rises steadily from Brighton to the Dyke, nearly 760 feet in 5.75 miles, so that the journey occupies about an hour.' Victorians visited Mr Booth's Museum of British Birds where they paid an admission charge of one shilling to see the birds that had been shot by Mr Booth before being mounted in cases representing the scene where they were taken. The same newspaper wrote: 'They consequently afford a most instructive illustration of the home and habits of birds.'

Since the 1930s, with the advent of the bus from Brighton to Devil's Dyke, train services soon became a thing of the past. Today, the No. 77 bus from Brighton takes just 15 minutes and an open-top bus is available on Sundays and bank holidays for tourists to 'Breeze up to the Dyke'.

Amongst those who have enjoyed the views are artists John Ruskin and Constable. Royal visitors were King William IV and Queen Adelaide with more than 50 carriages! Later on, the young, single Queen Victoria rode on horseback from the Pavilion, Brighton, up to the Dyke. After her marriage to Prince Albert, he accompanied her on a number of occasions.

Many years later, the Duke and Duchess of York visited the Dyke. The stone Royal Seat (*page 10*) commemorates the opening by the Duke, (later King George VI) who 'dedicated the Dyke Estate to the use of the public for ever on the 30th May 1928'.

Nowadays, hang-gliders enjoy the thrill of free flight over the Weald, school children love exploring mysterious lumps and bumps and the Dyke continues to delight us as much as ever.

Fact File:

Devil's Dyke is just north of Brighton and south of Hurstpierpoint.

'Mad Jack' Fuller of Brightling and his follies

'Mad Jack' Fuller, Georgian squire, philanthropist and MP at the start of the 19th century was a larger than life character remembered for his good deeds and the larger than life follies he left behind in Brightling, East Sussex.

Brightling is a quiet hamlet situated five miles north east of Battle with views towards the North and South Downs and the sea at Pevensey. It is also the home of many Fuller 'follies', structures built just for pleasure – not least the 'Egyptian' pyramid dwarfing the church of St Thomas – but more about that later!

Born John Fuller on 20th February 1757 in North Stoneham, Southampton, Hampshire, he was the only son of the Reverend Henry Fuller and his wife (and cousin) Frances, née Fuller. He spent his first few years in Hampshire with his parents and two sisters before moving to Sussex where, in 1761, his father died. John was four at the time. Six years later, he was sent to Eton College, Berkshire to complete his education.

Fuller's bust.

The Fuller family were influential landowners with several members active in politics. The family motto *carbone et forcipibus* ('By charcoal and tongs') aptly described their two main sources of wealth: ironworks and sugar plantations in the West Indies. The Fullers owned an iron furnace at Heathfield, where guns and cannons of all sizes were made for the Royal Navy, and the forge at Burwash Weald where a variety of tools were produced. In Jamaica, they owned large sugar plantations worked by slave labour before the abolition of slavery.

When John's uncle, Rose Fuller MP, died in 1777, he left the 20-year-old-John his immense wealth. Overnight John not only became the squire of Brightling, inheriting the family estate at Rose Hill Estate, now Brightling Park, but also the absentee owner of his Jamaican plantations.

During his lifetime, he had a chequered career. He was captain of a light infantry company in the Sussex Militia, later leading a troop when the threat of a Napoleonic invasion was at its height. Afterwards he entered the world of politics, from 1780 to 1784, when he was elected MP for Southampton. He was also High Sheriff of Sussex in 1796.

Sociable, with a loud, booming voice, he enjoyed playing cards, wagers and good food and wine, which inevitably led to his weight ballooning to a massive 22 stone and the nickname 'hippo'. He was also known as 'Mad Jack' and 'Honest John', the latter being the name he preferred to be known by. A down to earth Englishman, it is rumoured that when he was offered a peerage, he declined declaring: 'I was born Jack Fuller and Jack Fuller I will die!'

His friends included many notable figures of the day, such as the architect Sir Robert Smirke and the famous Sussex landscape painter J.M.W. Turner. But despite his popularity, he was not lucky in love. In 1790, aged 33, he tried his hand at marriage by proposing to Miss Susannah Thrale, then in her twenties but she turned him down and he remained a bachelor for the rest of his life.

From 1801 to 1812, he was MP for Sussex, but the life of a politician was at odds with his rough, outspoken character. On 30th May 1804, he was embroiled in a heated debate with anti-slave trade campaigner William Wilberforce. As a sugar plantation owner, he could see nothing wrong with slavery, even claiming that living conditions for slaves were equal to those of the labouring classes in England.

On the 27th February 1810, whilst drunk, he repeatedly interrupted the Earl of Chatham with thoughtless questions regarding the Walcheren Expedition the year before. He was ignored and on the orders of the Speaker, whom he addressed as 'the insignificant little fellow in the wig', the Serjeant-at-Arms and four messengers ejected his hefty frame from the chamber with great difficulty. However, after two days in custody he apologised and was let off with no more than a reprimand.

By 1812, he had had enough of his stormy political career, preferring to concentrate on his role as Squire of Brightling and the fine art of folly building. This was an expensive pursuit that only the very rich could afford, but it served another purpose. With unemployment very high during the early part of the 19th century, building follies provided the local population with a wage and relieved hardship, something 'Mad Jack' was keen to do.

His first folly, a temple with a 'mock Tudor' archway situated in the woods of Brightling Park, was built in 1803. Another folly dating between 1800–1820 stands not far from Brightling House in Brightling Park – a 12ft high pillar with a cast-iron flame and a canon and anchor on either side of it, possibly a reflection of the Fuller connection with the iron industry.

Between November 1810 and June 1811, he commissioned his future mausoleum, a 25ft high 'Egyptian' pyramid standing in St Thomas à Beckett's churchyard, Brightling. Apparently, the vicar gave him permission to build the pyramid only if he replaced the old public house with a new one half a mile away.

Rumours claimed 'Mad Jack' asked to be buried dressed for dinner wearing his top hat and seated at a table laden with a magnificent feast with a bottle of claret at his side and the floor covered with broken glass to keep the devil away. However, the rumours proved to be just that! When the pyramid was restored in 1983, it revealed that 'Mad Jack' was buried beneath the floor of the tomb in the traditional way.

Brightling is home to a number of other Fuller follies. Between 1810 and 1820 the upside down cone-shaped Sugar Loaf known as Fuller's Point was built, and named as such because, at the time, sugar was stored in a conical shape. Standing 35ft high on a 15ft circular base, it was built in one night using nothing more than mud and stones so that 'Mad Jack' could win a drunken wager with a friend that Dallington church spire was visible from Brightling Park. It was not, and he lost the wager.

The mausoleum in Brightling churchyard.

His largest project was the building of a four-mile wall around Brightling Park at a personal cost of £10,000, an enormous sum in those days. 'Mad Jack' paid labourers to build and maintain the 4ft–6ft high wall over a period of five to seven years with the bulk of the work carried out between 1815 and 1817.

He commissioned the building of the Observatory on top of the hill on the road from Brightling towards Burwash. Once a well-equipped, fully operational observatory, designed by Sir Robert Smirke in 1810 and completed in 1818, it reflects his genuine interest in astronomy. It also helped his loyal servants, who used a telescope in the observatory to keep an eye out for signs of his coach returning from London so that they could prepare a suitable welcome.

Another folly, the Watch Tower, is believed to have had two purposes. Jack could observe the restoration of Bodiam Castle, which he had bought for £3,000 at an auction in 1828 in order to save it from demolition, and it was a good lookout to warn of an attack from Napoleon's army.

Just outside Brightling stands Brightling Needle, a 65ft obelisk on Brightling Down. It is not known exactly when it was built or why, but the most likely reason is that it was used as a beacon point to warn of a possible invasion. Standing 646ft above sea level and at the second highest point in Sussex, it is used by the Ordnance Survey today.

In 1818, he used his great wealth to support and sponsor the Royal Institution, loaning them £10,000 (equivalent to approximately £100,000 today), which he later wrote off. He was a patron of the arts and science and gave the Institution two Fullerian Professorships in anatomy and physiology and chemistry. A marble bust of 'Mad Jack' stands in the Institution's grounds with the words: 'John Fuller, who gave ten thousand pounds for the promotion of science in the Royal Institution.'

As squire of Brightling, he supported the village church. In 1815, he had five bells at St Thomas à Beckett recast and a treble added in honour of the Duke of Wellington. A patriotic Englishman, he had the six bells inscribed with the names of each of the Duke of Wellington's last six battles – Tallavera, Salamanca, Vittoria, Pyrenees, Orthes and Toulouse. In 1818, he added two more bells inscribed 'Waterloo', making a peal of eight, and two years later he gave the church the largest barrel organ in the country, with a gallery to support it.

His generosity extended to Eastbourne, where he paid for the restoration of St Mary's Church. He turned his attention to helping those at sea when he gave Eastbourne a lifeboat and commissioned the building of the Belle Tout Lighthouse on the cliffs at Beachy Head, near Eastbourne, in 1831.

In 1834, at the age of 77 years, John Fuller died at his home in Devonshire Place in London. Typically, he chose to be buried in his Egyptian pyramid built

24 years earlier in the churchyard amongst his own people rather than on his own estate.

More recently this eccentric, generous and colourful character was remembered in 1997 when Brooke Bond PG Tips celebrated his achievements on card no. 43 of the Pyramid Power series of collectors' cards. In addition to this, there is a yearly reminder of his name through the energetic performances of Jack's Morris Dancers based in Hastings, East Sussex.

Over the years, the Sussex Historic Gardens Restoration Society has maintained the Fuller Follies, thus ensuring an enduring legacy to John Fuller, affectionately remembered as 'Mad Jack'.

Fact File:

Brightling in East Sussex is 5 miles north east of Battle. The tomb of 'Mad Jack' is in the churchyard at Brightling.

William Borrer's birthplace in Henfield.

William Borrer,
famous 19th century botanist of Henfield

William Borrer, the famous 19th century botanist, was born in Potwell, Henfield, West Sussex on 13th June, 1781. Shortly afterwards his father, William Borrer I, a landowner, corn merchant and occasional high sheriff of Sussex, his mother Mary and his two younger brothers moved to Pakyns Manor, a 16th century country house in Hurstpierpoint overlooking the South Downs.

As a boy, William's wealthy land-owning parents chose to send him to private schools in Hurstpierpoint, West Sussex, and Carshalton in Surrey. He left school early but continued studying French, theology and the classics under private tutors.

After school, despite wishing to study medicine, William assisted his father with his farming business, supplying forage to large numbers of troops and their horses stationed in Sussex during the early 19th century. At the time, England feared a large-scale French invasion from Napoleon 'Little Boney' Bonaparte, who was sweeping across Europe. With no reliable postal system or other form of communication, the young, thoughtful Borrer was the messenger travelling on horseback on his solitary rides throughout Sussex. At the same time, encouraged by the officers he met, he took the opportunity to note as many different plants as possible, considering no trouble too great to confirm his discovery.

Later on he became friends with other botanists of the age, such as Sir Joseph Banks, Dawson Turner and W. J. Hooker. In 1810, Borrer travelled with Hooker to Scotland and also to Normandy in France. He undertook many plant-hunting trips throughout Britain in search of species reported in new locations, remaining vigilant for any new discoveries. Specimens found were reliably named but often lacked a date or locality.

Borrer lived at Pakyns Manor, Hurstpierpoint, until his marriage at the age of 29. On 28th May 1810, he married Elizabeth, the daughter of banker Nathaniel Hall of Southwick. The newlyweds lived with William Borrer Senior while he built them a house in Henfield, overlooking the River Adur and favoured by wealthy people for their retirement.

From 19th December 1811, Barrow Hill, otherwise known as 'The Snake House' by the locals, was the Borrer matrimonial home, supported by a generous yearly allowance of £650 from his father. The marriage produced thirteen children but the couple suffered great tragedy when five of them died in infancy, leaving five daughters and three sons.

William Borrer's grave under a yew tree in St Peter's churchyard, Henfield.

Whilst pursuing his interest in botany, Borrer established a remarkable collection of living plants. By the autumn of 1860, assisted by his gardener Charles Green, he had as many as 6,600 different species and varieties in his garden. Barrow Hill (demolished in 1948 and now the site of Mill Drive and Cedar Way Estate) stood on a fruitful sandy ridge, a soil considered ideal for one of the best collections of plants ever grown in the English climate.

He contributed to The Bromfield Herbarium and formed his own herbarium rich in the flora of Sussex. On his death, his widow gave his herbarium to Kew. The herbarium was very comprehensive, due to Borrer's hard work and generosity in sharing his knowledge with others who, in turn, gave him plant specimens to add to his collection. Letters and papers to and from him are held in Kew Gardens Archives.

William Borrer tried to cultivate every critical British species together with as many exotic plants as possible. He had a considerable interest in the British genera Salix (willows), Rubus (blackberries and raspberries) and Rosa (roses). A great letter writer, he exchanged letters with Charles Darwin and contributed to numerous journals throughout his life. His first contribution in Turner and Dillwyn's *Botanist's Guide* 1805 was a comprehensive list of and critical notes on Sussex flowering plants, ferns, fungi, lichens and algae, along with some records for Kent, Surrey and Hampshire.

Borrer identified 21 species of flowering plants located from Cornwall to Caithness. During his travels, he discovered several rare seaweeds and carried out work on ferns, lichens and algae, combining precise description with methodical detail.

Often described as the father of British lichenology, he was considered an expert on British plants and lichen, having collected specimens from locations as varied as Cambridgeshire, Anglesey, Coventry, Devon, Sussex, Surrey, Suffolk, Morayshire, Guernsey, Yarmouth, Saffron Walden, Thetford and Hastings.

On 3rd December 1805 Borrer was elected a Fellow of the Linnean Society. In 1810, he became a member of the Wernerian Natural History Society and on 4th June 1835 he was elected a Fellow of the Royal Society. In 1842, he was elected a Fellow of the Botanical Society of Edinburgh, and several plants were also named after him.

A philanthropist in his own quiet way, Borrer used his considerable personal wealth for the benefit of others, making charitable contributions to the Henfield community, particularly in the field of education. In 1812, he formed the Henfield Society for Educating the Poor, and from 1815 to 1855 there were 66 subscribers to the scheme. After 1819 he built a school for girls, and in 1844 a school for infants was built on his own land.

Conscientious and caring, he undertook the education of three or four boys and found them employment when they had completed their education. In addition to this, Borrer served as a justice of the peace for Sussex and, at his own expense, enlarged the church and provided an endowment for its clergy.

On 10th January 1862 William Borrer died at his home, Barrow Hill, Henfield from pleurisy, having suffered from ill health for the last decade of his life.

In the Parham Chapel of St Peter's Church there is a window dedicated to Borrer's life, and in the north-east corner of St Peter's churchyard, beside a yew bush, are the worn and faded gravestones bearing the names of William Borrer and other members of the Borrer family.

Fact File:

Henfield Museum, Henfield Hall, Coopers Way, High Street, Henfield, BN5 9DB. Tel: 01273 492507.

The Parnell family grave in Littlehampton.

The Sussex Love Story of Charles Stewart Parnell and 'Kitty' O'Shea

When Charles Stewart Parnell, the M.P. known as 'the uncrowned King of Ireland' fell in love with Katharine Wood, the couple tied the knot in Steyning on 25th June 1891. However, this was no ordinary marriage but one shrouded in political scandal on a grand scale.

Why, you may wonder. It had all started years before. Katharine was born in 1845 in Essex. Her father was Sir John Page Wood, 2nd baronet; her brother became Field Marshal Sir Evelyn Wood; and her uncle was Lord Hatherley, Prime Minister Gladstone's first Liberal lord chancellor. She was an upper class Victorian girl who loved music and embroidery and housecraft, but most of all she wanted to get married and have a family.

With this aim in mind, she married Captain William 'Willie' O'Shea in 1867. He was well connected, with a pedigree that matched her own. He was also a descendant of the old Norman aristocracy who had colonised Ireland in the 12th century, and therefore he appeared a suitable match by Victorian standards.

The couple set up home in Brighton and Patcham from 1870 and settled down to raise the three children who quickly followed. Shortly afterwards the young family moved to Eltham, South London, where O'Shea became the MP for Galway. He also became the aide to Parnell, the leader of Ireland's Home Rule movement.

Over the years Katharine's marriage to Willie had palled, and from 1875 she and her husband lived apart. Disenchanted, she described her life as 'narrow, narrow, narrow and so deadly dull'. To improve her lot, she moved to Sussex where, in 1883, she rented 39 Bedford Square, Brighton, and later Medina Terrace in Hove, while still spending time in Eltham for the sake of appearances.

Five years had passed since her separation when, in 1880, Katharine met the unmarried, debonair Parnell for the first time through her family connections with the Liberal Party. There were many opportunities to see him during negotiations prior to the introduction of the First Irish Home Rule Bill in 1886, when she liased regularly between Parnell and Prime Minister Gladstone. She also socialised with the handsome bachelor at dinner parties in Berkeley Square, during which time Parnell sent her love letters addressing her as 'Dearest love'.

Her marriage to Willy was an empty shell, and she welcomed Parnell into her home in Eltham, Surrey, much to the fury of her estranged husband. O'Shea not only forbade Katharine to see Parnell but he also challenged him to a duel. However, Katharine's wealthy 'Aunt Ben' (Mrs Benjamin Wood) supported Katharine financially, and O'Shea chose to keep quiet about the affair.

Katharine and Parnell continued to live together as a married couple in all but name. Three children were born, but their first daughter, Claude Sophie, died in 1882 aged just three months. Two more daughters followed, Claire (1883–1909) and Katharine (1884–1947). O'Shea still refused to give Katharine the divorce she longed for, believing that wealthy Aunt Ben would leave her a large inheritance from which he would benefit indirectly. However, Aunt Ben had her own ideas, and when she died in 1889 at the age of 95 she left her money in trust to her cousins, thus ensuring that O'Shea would not get a penny.

For O'Shea this was the final straw. With no chance of a financial gain, he filed for divorce on 24th December 1889, citing Parnell (then at the height of his popularity) as co-respondent. Matters quickly escalated when on 15th November, 1890, the case came to trial and Parnell was exposed to the press and the eyes of the world as the long-term lover and father of three of Katharine's children.

Victorians were affronted, expecting Parnell to at least challenge O'Shea's allegations. But Parnell refused to disagree with O'Shea in any way, seeing it as his chance to achieve his dearest dream of marrying Katharine.

Two days later, on 17th November, a divorce decree was granted. But that was not the end of the matter. Parnell was promptly deposed as leader of the Irish Parliamentary Party, and Gladstone distanced himself by withdrawing his support, claiming that home rule for Ireland was impossible if Parnell remained. Katharine was dubbed 'Kitty', Victorian slang for a prostitute, and the churches of Ireland, once very much in favour of Parnell, poured scorn on him.

More disapproval followed. Cartoons and music halls mocked Katharine, and pubs were named 'Kitty O'Shea' portraying her as an immoral and bawdy woman, a description that could not have been further from the truth. Loyal friends spoke of her intelligence, her charming manner and her wish to do nothing more than care for Parnell and their children. But this support was ignored. For the 'crime' of divorcing her first husband in order to marry Charles Parnell, the leader of Ireland's Home Rule movement, she was blamed for Parnell's failure and never forgiven.

Ignoring the furore, Katharine and Parnell and their two surviving children moved to 10 Walsingham Terrace, Hove, in 1889. Two years later, on 25th June 1891, the couple travelled by horse and carriage to Steyning, the ancient market town under the South Downs, for their longed-for marriage. As an added precaution, to throw the press off the scent, Katharine's faithful maid and elderly nurse travelled by train to act as witnesses in Steyning register office, then known as Osborne House.

No church wedding had been possible. All local vicars had refused to marry the couple because divorce was unacceptable to the straight-laced Victorians. Fortunately Mr Cripps, the registrar in Steyning, had no such qualms. For the civil service Katharine wore white roses pinned to her dress. Parnell, observed Mr Cripps, was 'one of the happiest bridegrooms I had ever married'.

The house in Steyning once used as a register office.

When the newly-weds returned to their home, a scrum of reporters awaited them. Some hours later, with no chance of an interview, the press eventually left, giving the Parnell's the chance to walk peacefully along the promenade in the evening for the first time as a married couple.

After his marriage, Parnell returned to the exhausting life of an Irish public agitator, where he fought the third and last by-election in Co. Carlow. But such was public disapproval that, whilst campaigning, angry crowds assaulted him and threw quicklime into his eyes.

He refused to be cowed, and on 27th September, in pouring rain and fragile health, he addressed a crowd at Creggs on the Galway-Roscommon border.

Shortly afterwards, he contracted pneumonia. Desperately ill, he returned to Katharine and his home in Brighton only to lapse into unconsciousness. On 6th October 1891 he died of a heart attack in his wife's arms, just 45 years old.

Katharine never recovered from her loss. She struggled to pick up the pieces of her life, writing two volumes, *Charles Stewart Parnell: his Love Story* and *Political Life* in 1914. Norah, her daughter by O'Shea, lived with Katharine and cared for her until her death in 1921 in Littlehampton. Two years later, Norah died and was buried in the same plot.

In 2003, the Parnell Society laid a granite stone at the foot of Katharine's grave with the inscription: *'I will give my life to Ireland but to you I give my love.' C.S Parnell (1846–91).*

Katharine and Parnell's love affair shook two nations, but there could be no more fitting and enduring epitaph.

Fact File:

Steyning is located 4 miles north of Shoreham in the Horsham district of West Sussex. Littlehampton is on the south coast between Portsmouth and Brighton.

Blood, Sweat and Tears
on the Balcombe Viaduct

It would be hard to find a more magnificent Victorian railway structure than the Balcombe Ouse Valley Viaduct, which today carries thousands of rail commuters on the London to Brighton line in Sussex.

Designed by the engineer John Urpeth Rastrick in conjunction with the architect David Mocatta for the London and Brighton Railway, it is considered one of the most elegant viaducts in the country.

The structure was built over the River Ouse from 1839 to 1841 as part of the original London to Brighton line, including the nearby Balcombe tunnel and tunnels at Merstham, Haywards Heath, Clayton and Patcham. It is 1,475ft (450m) long with 37 semi-circular brick arches with pierced piers. Each arch is 37ft wide and the tallest is 97ft high.

Engineering Timelines records that 'The piers are tapered both sides and end-on and divided in two by 10ft wide weight-saving voids, which are capped by six-ring brick arches. Thus the whole has a slender appearance.'

A modern train speeds over the Balcombe Viaduct.

David Mocatta designed the eight classical stone and brick pavilions, four on each end and a stone balustrade on the viaduct. The viaduct is probably one of the finest examples of the Victorian railway system. It not only looks impressive, but it connected Sussex and the Sussex coast with London quickly and efficiently for the first time.

Red bricks were imported from Holland. The bricks and all the materials were transported by barge up the then navigable Ouse (now no more than a stream in many places) via Lewes and the port of Newhaven 25 miles away. This was no mean feat, as the viaduct was constructed using 11 million bricks!

By the mid 19th century horse drawn stagecoaches had been replaced by railway mania, then at its height. Huge armies of labourers – navvies – travelled the country looking for rail construction work. More than 250,000 navvies throughout Britain worked on railway constructions such as the Balcombe Viaduct, with one in every 100 persons employed as a navvy.

Navvies were a tough breed of Irish immigrants, Scots and men from Lancashire and Yorkshire. They were capable of undertaking physically demanding and dangerous work such as the construction of the Balcombe Viaduct, working in all weathers using picks, shovels, a wheelbarrow and a barrel of gunpowder.

Hardened navvies could move up to 20 tonnes of earth a day working long hours at greater and greater speeds, with little regard for their personal safety. Local farm labourers were very rarely recruited, as they were not strong enough, and inexperienced navvies often worked for half a day at first until they had built up enough stamina for longer hours. The work was so physically demanding that the men ate enormous meals to keep up their energy, something the contractors were quick to exploit by selling them food at inflated prices.

The navvies, some accompanied by their wives and children, gathered in huge groups by or near the railway under construction, living in shanty towns and primitive cabins capable of sleeping up to twenty men. Others lived in improvised shelters of mud, timber and tarpaulins, whilst some slept in the open air. The on-line History Learning Site describes how navvies who slept in a bed paid approximately one and half pennies per night, whilst those who chose to sleep on the floor would pay much less – one penny for five nights.

Some navvies found lodgings in local villages, often to the dismay of the locals. When 'going on a randy' – navvy slang for getting drunk – they also swore like navvies, something that displeased the local community who feared their rough and ready ways.

They were employed by contractors responsible for the whole line or sub-contractors building a section of the route. Alternatively, 'gangers' might employ them, sometimes on a day rate or for an agreed piecework price. The work paid much more than factory jobs and twice that of farm work. Once a month they received their wages from the local pub, an arrangement that suited the publican but no one else. Womanizing, swearing and accidents on the job followed, making them even more unpopular with the locals. Many navvies died in their early 40s as a result of the harsh nature of the work.

The Balcombe Viaduct opened when the Norwood Junction–Haywards Heath section was completed on 12th July 1841. The second section of the line between London and Brighton was completed in September 1841. It took over three years, 3,500 men and 570 horses to build the entire London to Brighton railway at a cost of £2,634,059 (£57,262 per mile). During this time a thousand navvies, some with families, set up camp in and around the villages of Balcombe, Cuckfield, Ardingly, Horsted Keynes and Lindfield.

The impact of the new Brighton–London line was so great that between 1841 and 1871 large numbers of people moved to Brighton, resulting in the population swelling from 46,661 to 90,011. The quick and relatively cheap third class travel in open-topped rail carriages enabled 360,000 people to travel to Brighton by train in 1843.

After the last war, there was a period of neglect until the 1980s. This was remedied when the British Railways Board established the Railway Heritage

Railtrack Plc repaired and restored the viaduct between 1996 and 1999 with grants from the Railway Heritage Trust and English Heritage.

Trust in 1985 in an effort to preserve Britain's Victorian railway heritage. Railtrack Plc repaired and restored the viaduct between 1996 and 1999 with grants from the Railway Heritage Trust and English Heritage. The original stone from Caen in Normandy had been exhausted; therefore matching stone was imported from Auxerre in France to repair the existing balustrades and pavilions, all without disrupting the trains travelling across the viaduct.

On 8th May 1983, the Balcombe Viaduct was made a Grade II listed building. A working viaduct, some 220 modern high-speed trains pass over the Ouse Valley every day giving commuters some of the best views of Sussex, all made possible by the navvies who worked on it through blood, sweat and tears.

Fact File:

The Balcombe Viaduct is between Balcombe and Haywards Heath.

Bishop James Hannington, Sussex Martyr of Hurstpierpoint

James Hannington, the English missionary known as the Sussex Martyr, was born on 3rd September 1847 at St George's in Hurstpierpoint under the Downs.

The son of Colonel Charles Smith Hannington, and grandson of Smith Hannington, founder of the Hanningtons store in Brighton, his family were wealthy landowners. In 1852, Colonel Hannington built an Independent chapel, known as Little Park Chapel, in the grounds of St George's, the Hannington family home. However, when the family returned to the Church of England in 1867, the chapel did too, and was then known as St George's Church.

Active and full of fun, James was 12 when he blew up a wasp's nest with gunpowder, causing him to lose his left thumb in the process. Later, at Temple School in Brighton, he was popular with his fellow students, earning him the nickname 'Mad Jim'. A poor scholar, he left school aged 15 to work in his father's business in Brighton, but after six years he decided the business world was not for him.

St George's House, Hurstpierpoint.

As a young man, Hannington enjoyed sailing, riding, shooting, athletic sports and travelling extensively across Europe. In 1864, he joined the 1st Sussex Artillery Volunteers, quickly becoming a major in 1866. However, two years later he decided to become an Anglican clergyman, entering university at St Mary's Hall, Oxford, where he was awarded his Bachelor of Arts degree.

In 1874 Hannington was ordained at Exeter Cathedral as a deacon. He took charge of the small parishes of Martinhoe and Trentishoe in Devon, where he was much loved and respected. The little churches were packed, sometimes even overflowing into the porch and churchyard. When not preaching, he supported his parishioners both practically and spiritually by riding his Exmoor pony from cottage to cottage over rough moors and wild cliffs in all weathers. Yet despite his dedication, he harboured a deep dissatisfaction that he had not experienced what he preached at first hand.

A turning point was when his college friend, Rev. E.C. Dawson, sent him the book *Grace and Truth* by Dr W.P. Mackay. Deeply affected by what he had read, he wrote: ' . . . from that day to this I have lived under the shadow of His wings in the assurance that I am His and He is mine'.

On 29th September 1875, at the instigation of his father, Colonel Hannington, he became curate-in-charge of St George's Church, Hurstpierpoint. He left his Devon parish with mixed feelings, having grown to love the people and the wild, windswept Devon landscape. Two years later, on 10th February 1877, he married Blanche Hankin-Turvin, a member of St George's congregation, and the couple went on to have three children in four years.

He was tall, well built with clear grey eyes and a beard, and his parishioners listened attentively as 'Jemmy' preached against the temptations of drink offered by the seven public houses in Hurstpierpoint at that time. Advocating total abstinence, 'the old fuddlers' – those over fond of alcohol – were regularly waylaid. 'Ah! You're another old fuddler; won't you come and write in my little book?' – he would say referring to his pledge-book, which he carried wherever he went. If that failed, other inducements were meetings and bible classes in the mission room with tea and cakes!

In 1882, having heard about the murder of two missionaries on the shores of the Victoria Nyanza, he left his wife and three children in England, believing it would be 'homicide' to take them – a belief that later proved prophetic. He sailed for Zanzibar, where he joined the Church Missionary Society in East Africa in charge of six missionaries, but a year later fever and dysentery forced him to return to Sussex.

His health improved, and in June 1884 the Church Missionary Society arranged with the Archbishop of Canterbury that he should be ordained as the first bishop of Eastern Equatorial Africa. He sailed again, arriving at Frere Town near Mombasa, Kenya, on 24th January 1885 determined to open up a new, shorter route to Uganda.

With his caravan of about 200 porters and Mr Jones, an African clergyman and former slave, the party eventually reached a spot near Victoria Nyanza. After enduring much hardship, Hannington left Mr Jones and most of the party to continue to the north-east of the lake for the final leg of the trip.

Sadly, King Mwanga II of Buganda viewed the bishop and his fifty porters with great hostility, as they had entered his country through the 'back door', traditionally the route taken by the king's enemies.

King Mwanga ordered Busoga chiefs to imprison Hannington and his men in Busoga, where they were held in captivity for eight days. During this time Hannington wrote a daily account of his last days in his small diary. On the seventh day, he wrote: 'A terrible night, first with noisy drunken guard, and secondly with vermin, which have found out my tent and swarm.' On his last night, weakened by fever and nearly delirious, he drew comfort from Psalm 37 in his Prayer Book.

On 29th October 1885 Hannington was led towards the banks of the Victoria Nile, where some accounts say he was shot with his own rifle while others describe how he was speared in both sides. His alleged last words to his attackers were: 'Go, tell Mwanga I have purchased the road to Uganda with my blood.' He was just 38 years old.

JAMES HANNINGTON D.D.
Born here at St George's 1847
First Bishop of
Eastern Equatorial Africa
Killed at Lake Victoria 1885
Evangelist & Martyr
HURSTPIERPOINT SOCIETY

Most of Hannington's men were speared to death, but four managed to escape to return to the original party, where they broke the news of the murder of the bishop and his men. Later, Joseph Mukasa, a Roman Catholic priest, and an official in Mwanga's court, rebuked the king for his murderous acts and was promptly beheaded for it.

The bishop did not die in vain. James Hannington and his companions were the first martyrs of Uganda: his Feast Day, with its special prayer, is 29th October. The Hannington Memorial Chapel in Namirembe Cathedral, Kampala, Uganda, and the Bishop Hannington Memorial Church in Hove are named in his honour.

Fact File:

Hurstpierpoint is north of Brighton and south of Burgess Hill. The nearest railway station is Hassocks.

School Founder Canon Nathaniel Woodard of Henfield

Canon Nathaniel Woodard of Henfield is remembered as the founder of Lancing, Hurstpierpoint and Ardingly Colleges and seven others all with the same ethos: 'Faith, Unity and Vision'.

Woodard's own education was very different from the schools he founded. Born the ninth of twelve children in 1811, he was the son of an impoverished farmer, and his mother, a devout Church of England woman, educated her children at the family home, Basildon Hall in Essex.

When he was 23 his two aunts enabled him to study at Magdalen Hall, Oxford University, where he was influenced by the Tracterian movement. Half way through his course he married his wife, Elizabeth Harriet Brill, and by the time he graduated in 1840 three of his eight children had been born. It took him six years to obtain a BA pass degree.

Lancing College Chapel.

After his ordination by the Bishop of London, Charles J. Blomfield in 1841, he became the curate in-charge of St Bartholomew's in Bethnal Green, East London. The parish was very poor, and Woodard worked hard to raise enough funds to complete the church, equip the school and educate his children.

He was popular with his parishioners, but in 1843 he preached a controversial sermon commending the use of confession and absolution. Some parishioners complained to the bishop, while others wrote to national newspapers supporting him. He was condemned by the bishop for his 'erroneous and dangerous notions' and forced to resign.

This led to influential friends securing him a post in the wilderness of St Mary's de Houra (of the Harbour) in New Shoreham, Sussex, in 1846. By this time he had been married for ten years, five of his eight children had been born – two died very young, and another son died aged 19 – and he had become aware that the middle classes were not receiving the benefits of a good education.

On 11th January 1847 Woodard founded St Mary's Grammar School in the dining room of New Shoreham vicarage, where he taught reading, writing, arithmetic, religious instruction, navigation, land surveying and book-keeping, all for just 15 shillings a quarter.

Woodard's home in Henfield, Martyn Lodge.

A few months later, in March 1848, he published a pamphlet *A Plea for the Middle Classes*, outlining his wish to provide the lower, middle and upper middle classes with a sound Christian education 'at such a charge as will make it available to most of them'. The pamphlet was widely read and became very influential.

Woodard leased properties in and around Shoreham, opening Shoreham Grammar School and Collegiate Institution for boarders, including his own sons, in August 1848. Four years later he bought Burwells and Malthouse Farms on the South Downs for the purpose of building the school that eventually became Lancing College in 1857.

Other Sussex schools were established through Woodard's extraordinary fund-raising skills, hard work, ceaseless correspondence and dynamic personality. His proposals created great interest. By 1855 he had collected approximately £40,000 for Hurstpierpoint, and a few years later he raised £30,000 for Lancing College and Lancing Chapel.

Woodard allocated most of the money for buildings set in beautiful locations, employing the eminent architects R.C. Carpenter, his son 'young Carpenter' and William Slater for Lancing Chapel, his outstanding legacy to the nation. He declared: 'No system of education would be perfect which did not provide for the cultivation of the taste of the pupils through the agency of the highest examples of architecture.'

Hurstpierpoint College was founded in 1849, followed by Ardingly College in 1858, where the fees were just £15.00 per annum, enabling the lower middle classes to attend – a cause dear to Woodard's heart.

Funds were raised through pamphlets and circulars, subscriptions, school events, popular breakfast parties and 'nice luncheons' for trustees such as Lord Salisbury who commented: 'The definition of a trustee is a luncheon-eating animal.' Supporters included politicians, bankers, the aristocracy and archbishops from Woodard's time in London. On one occasion, before a fund-raising luncheon, Woodward announced forcefully: 'Gentlemen, you do not use this room until you have contributed £10,000.' All granted his wish!

In 1870 Oxford University granted him an honorary Doctor of Civil Law (DCL), and in the same year Prime Minister Gladstone made him a canon of Manchester Cathedral with a stipend of £2,000 a year, most of which went to developing boys' schools. However, in 1855, despite his feelings about 'these fancy schools set up for girls', he helped a female friend develop St Michael's School for Girls, which later became a Woodard school. These were followed by St Anne's School (1874), St Mary's School (1880), both in Abbots Bromley, and St Winifred's School (1887) in Bangor.

His salary as provost of all his schools made him a wealthy man, but years of administration, school affairs and fundraising had weakened him. In 1862, 'in a fallen and helpless state', he retired to Henfield, where he lived in Martyn Lodge, a large country house near St Peter's church and The Cat House, home of George Ward.

The story goes that Woodard's cat killed George Ward's canary. This infuriated Ward, who painted his thatched cottage with pictures of a cat holding a bird, shook strings of sea-shells and rigged up a black figure which would appear ominously at a small window called the Zulu hole as the canon made his way to St Peter's church.

Widowed since 1873 and suffering from declining mental and physical health, the 78-year-old canon married Dorothy Louisa Porritt, the 23-year-old daughter of schoolmaster Benjamin Porritt on January 8th 1890. Fifteen months later Woodard died at his home, Martyn Lodge, on 25th April 1891. Five days later, on 30th April, his funeral took place in Lancing Chapel – the chapel he had founded, and the fourth tallest ecclesiastical building in the country.

At the time of his death, he had founded three girls' schools and eight boys' schools, and he and his supporters had raised at least £500,000. His dream lives on, and today there are 37 Woodard schools in England and Wales, one in Australia, one in America and one in Malawi.

Fact File:

Ardingly College is just outside Ardingly; Hurstpierpoint College, College Lane Hurstpierpoint; Lancing College, Lancing, West Sussex. Henfield is 12 miles northwest of Brighton.

'Dr Brighton' and Wounded Indian Soldiers of the Great War

'Dr Brighton' was the term first coined during the Regency era when Brighton was known as a health resort for the rich. However, in the autumn of 1914 local newspapers wrote once more that Dr Brighton would be treating 'Indian Warriors' wounded on the front at the Royal Pavilion and other locations in the town.

Local people were intrigued. It all started on 8th August 1914 when Indian troops left India to serve as reservists in Egypt due to a shortage of Allied forces in North Africa, the Middle East and Europe. Fighting on the Western Front had become so fierce that the Indians, still dressed in lightweight khaki uniforms suitable for Egypt, found themselves facing the colder climate of France and the ferocity of the well-equipped, well-trained German army.

Following their arrival in Marseilles on 26th September 1914, casualties started mounting up alarmingly, making it impossible to find nearby hospital accommodation behind the battle lines. Alternative arrangements were made, and wounded Indian troops were redirected to southern England, with offers of medical treatment from East Brockenhurst, New Milton, Southampton, Bournemouth and Brighton.

King George V heard of their plight and immediately requested that the Royal Pavilion be used as a military hospital for wounded Indian soldiers. The

Indian soldiers at the Royal Pavilion. By kind permission of
www.black-history.org.uk

request was granted by Sir John Otter, the mayor at the time, and consultations between the chairman of the pavilion committee and the town clerk followed. In November 1914 an urgent telegram was sent to Lord Kitchener, the secretary of state for war: 'Understanding that the Royal Pavilion at Brighton is specially suited for hospital treatment of Indian troops, the corporation beg to place it at His Majesty's disposal for that purpose.'

Just 24 hours later, the Royal Pavilion had been completely dismantled ready for the alterations necessary, with every effort made to avoid conflicts and ensure a harmonious atmosphere among the different races, castes and religions.

Just a week later the first Indian patients moved in, with the three main religions (Muslim, Sikh and Hindu) being given every consideration. Soldiers of different religions were treated in the same wards, and therefore two drinking taps were provided – one for Muslims and one for Hindus. A marquee was erected in the Pavilion grounds as a Sikh temple, and the Muslims were allocated the lawn in front of the Dome for worship, facing east towards Mecca. Nine kitchens were set up in huts on the lawns to cater for the different styles of cooking and religious beliefs, and special arrangements were made for the ritual killing of animals and the storing of meat.

The new role of the Pavilion caused great curiosity, particularly among the women of Brighton. The decision was made to surround the Pavilion grounds with palisades and wooden screens, but this did not deter some of the more energetic women from scrambling on top of the fences in order to glimpse the soldiers recuperating in the gardens – 'certainly not an edifying spectacle', tut-tutted the authorities.

Other buildings converted into Indian military hospitals were the Dome, the Corn Exchange, the Work House in Elm Grove (renamed the Kitchener General Indian Hospital and later to become Brighton General Hospital) and York Place School, where there were operating theatres, X-ray departments and rooms suitable for heat and electrical treatment.

But getting to Dr Brighton was not easy. Many wounded soldiers were unable to return to their unit due to the severity of their wounds, so were forced to endure a long, cold wait in water-logged trenches until stretcher-bearers could rescue them under cover of dark. Many did not survive, but those who did faced transportation on one of six hospital trains to Boulogne or Le Havre and a voyage on a hospital ship to the south coast, after which they had to endure another trip by rail to Brighton railway station and a military hospital.

On December 5th 1914, the *Brighton Gazette* reported that a small number of wounded Indian soldiers had arrived at the Royal Pavilion, then known as the Pavilion Military Hospital. A week later, on 14th December, the *Gazette* proclaimed 'Oriental Patients for Dr Brighton' after two heavily laden trains trundled into Brighton with 345 injured Indian soldiers on board.

The welcoming party at Brighton railway station included the chief constable, the mayor, the Red Cross, St John Ambulance and scores of people ready to offer them packets of cigarettes and other gifts. Motor ambulances transported 160 stretcher cases to York Place Hospital and the Pavilion Military Hospital, whilst the walking wounded made their way on foot. Local newspapers wrote how these 'Sons of the East' straight from the Front Line walked from the station to the Pavilion Military Hospital in driving rain, while the locals lined the route to cheer them on and show their appreciation of their bravery in the Empire's time of need.

From 1914 to 1916 Dr Brighton treated over 12,000 wounded Indian soldiers. His team included British doctors and surgeons from the Indian Medical Service or Civil Medical Service in India who were able to speak Hindustani, and Anglo-Indian sub-assistant surgeons. Ward orderlies ensured that every need was met, including the provision of a clean bed with a good mattress – a luxury after mud-filled trenches. In the wards, the wounded soldiers enjoyed phonographs and pianos and regular deliveries of fruit and clothes.

Morale was kept up with trips to the pier to take in the Brighton sea air, picnics, motor car rides and concert performances in the Pavilion Music Room arranged by Colonel G.H. Brooke Coates, C.B., former commandant of the 25th Punjab Infantry. There were also garden parties thrown by wealthy Brightonians and regular donations of cigarettes and other 'comforts' from the locals.

The Royal Pavilion was renamed the Pavilion Military Hospital.

Perhaps the greatest highlight and morale booster of all were royal visits, such as when King George V and Queen Mary visited Brighton for a tour of the military hospitals in 1915. On 9th January 1915, the *Argus* reported the tremendous excitement in the town as crowds gathered outside the Royal Pavilion to catch a glimpse of 'the Royal motor-car' entering the gates of the Pavilion estate.

The *Argus* described '. . . the extraordinary eagerness and delighted expectancy depicted on the faces of the wounded Indians prior to the coming of the King-Emperor and the Queen, and the extremely gracious kindness of the Royal visitors in their demeanour towards their gallant Indian warriors.'

The standard of medical care was so high that the vast majority of Indian soldiers recovered. However, those that did not were buried or cremated with due regard for their religious customs. Muslims were buried in a mosque in Woking, and Hindus and Sikhs were taken to an open-air funeral pyre, a 'ghat', on the South Downs, the site of which later became the white dome of the Chattri, unveiled by the Prince of Wales on the 21st February 1921.

When the Indian soldiers left the Pavilion in 1916 the authorities gave the public the chance to see the wards and the special care the soldiers had received from Dr Brighton. From the first week of February, for a charge in aid of the mayor of Brighton's war charities, eager visitors roamed through the buildings and gardens, inspecting the different kitchens, the soldiers' beds and bedside tables, all in specially tidied wards, the praying tents and the Pavilion as an Indian hospital – something they had wondered about over the last two years.

Curiosity was so great, noted Joyce Collins in her book *Dr Brighton's Indian Patients December 1914–January 1916*, that '2,675 people queued right through Castle Square to the Steine to get in, passing the pay-box at a rate of 15 a minute'.

When the Indians returned to their small villages dotted across India, they spread the word regarding Dr Brighton's wonderful curative and healing powers, something they never forgot. As a mark of gratitude to the people of Brighton for nursing the wounded Indian soldiers back to good health, the Indian Memorial Gateway to the Royal Pavilion was erected.

On 26th October 1921, in a historic ceremony, Major-General His Highness the Maharajah of Patiala unveiled the memorial, and the mayor of Brighton, Councillor B.N. Southall reciprocated by presenting the maharaja with a copy of the original gold key to the Royal Pavilion.

The impressive gateway bears the following inscription: 'This gateway is the gift of India in commemoration of her sons who – stricken in the Great War – were tended in the Pavilion in 1914 and 1915. Dedicated to the use of the inhabitants of Brighton, B.N. Southall, Mayor.'

The White Dome of the Chattri, Memorial to Our Indian Comrades

On June 18th 2006, at 2.30pm, the 56th annual memorial service in honour of the Indian soldiers who died fighting for Britain in World War I took place at the white dome of the Chattri, the Indian monument nestling behind yellow gorse bushes on top of the Downs. The 30-minute service marked the 85th anniversary of the unveiling of the memorial on 1st February 1921 by 27-year-old Edward, Prince of Wales, later the Duke of Windsor.

Located 500 feet above sea level south of Ditchling Beacon and north of Patcham, the Chattri (meaning umbrella in Hindi, Punjabi and Urdu) denotes a cenotaph or empty tomb with an eight-sided base with eight pillars to support the dome. It was designed by E.C. Henriques, a young Indian Hindu architect, under the supervision of the British architect Sir Jacob Swinton. The monument, made of white Sicilian marble and approximately 2.7 metres wide and 8.8 metres high, was built and jointly funded by Brighton Corporation and the India Office. Originally it stood in 44 acres donated by the Marquis of Abergavenny, but today it stands in two acres of ground, where it is cared for by Brighton and Hove City Council.

After the 56th annual memorial service on 18th June, 2006.

The Chattri is built on the exact site where 53 Sikhs and Hindus who died from their wounds were cremated on funeral pyres – burning ghats – on the South Downs from 31st December 1914 to the 30th December 1915.

Every effort was made to observe the ritual of the burning ghats for the men who died alone and far from home in a foreign land and in a foreign conflict not of their making. The site chosen for the cremations was a secluded hollow far from the hustle and bustle of Brighton and the surrounding villages. Metals, grains, fruits, flowers and scents were used symbolically, and the low intermittent chanting of Vedic hymns could be heard drifting across the rolling farmland.

Afterwards, in accordance with recognised rites, the ashes were scattered at sea. Three massive granite plinths measuring 8ft by 4ft cover the original concrete crematory bases.

On the day of the unveiling there was an air of excitement as hundreds of cars, riders on horseback, spectators on foot and reporters from national and international newspapers climbed the hill to witness the occasion. According to the *Brighton Herald* on Saturday February 5th, 1921, amongst the local dignitaries around the Chattri was 'Rudyard Kipling, our story-teller of India and the poet of Empire.'

The royal party attempted to drive up by car. The wheels of the prince's Rolls Royce slipped in the wet grass of the steep hillside, and burly local men tried to haul the car out of the ruts with tow-ropes, but to no avail. Without

The Chattri.

hesitation Edward, dressed in khaki with the Welsh leek on the black band of his cap, walked towards the white dome gleaming in the distance past the cheering crowds, some standing on farm wagons for a better view.

The locals watched in silence as, with quiet dignity, the mayor of Brighton accompanied Prince Edward as he climbed the tiers of grey brown steps past the pillars rising from a granite base. An enormous flag bearing the emblem of India on a background of the Union Jack covered the Chattri. A soldier with bowed head leaning on the butt of his rifle stood at each of the four corners and soldiers in two ranks stood on the slope above the monument.

Once the Prince of Wales had unveiled the Chattri, he spoke of 'a memorial to brave men, our fellow subjects, who after the fire and stress of Flanders, received the last sacred rites of their religion on this high eminence'.

Following the Prince of Wales's address, soldiers at the top of the hill fired three volleys. Drums rolled then a hushed silence and the haunting sound of the Last Post. Finally, the reveille sounded symbolising new hope.

To mark the occasion, a sumptuous luncheon was arranged in the Banqueting Room of the Royal Pavilion. The Prince of Wales accepted a silver tablet engraved with a representation of the Chattri, and Rudyard Kipling and his fellow guests each received an illustrated souvenir of the ceremony.

The Chattri bears the following inscription in Hindi and English: 'To the memory of all the Indian soldiers who gave their lives for their King-Emperor in the Great War, this monument, erected on the site of the funeral pyre where the Hindus and Sikhs who died in hospital at Brighton, passed through the fire, is in grateful admiration and brotherly affection dedicated.'

Sadly, there was a period when the monument was neglected. But from 1950 to 1999, the Patcham branch of the Royal British Legion resurrected the annual memorial service, until advancing years and dwindling membership made it impossible to continue.

Since June 2000 Mr Davinder Dhillon, a local Sikh teacher in conjunction with the Undivided Indian Ex-Services Association, has organised the service – believed to be the only one of its kind in Britain.

In September 2010 a new memorial was raised next to the Chattri. It honours 53 Indian soldiers who died during the 1914–18 conflict, and was created by stonemasons from the Commonwealth War Graves Commission.

Fact File:

The Chattri is located on the South Downs near Patcham and can only be reached on foot.

Danny at Hurstpierpoint.

Danny, Lloyd George
and the Armistice Talks

Danny, the dignified mansion at the foot of the Sussex Downs, is a fine example of Elizabethan architecture. Secluded, with distinctive Tudor red bricks, gabled roofs and tall mullion windows, it is a house with a fascinating and varied past. Most significantly, it was here, in 1918, that the imperial war cabinet of World War I met in secret to discuss the terms for the Armistice talks leading to the conclusion of the Great War.

Situated between the villages of Hurstpierpoint and Hassocks, down a sheltered lane, Danny is surrounded by the fields and woods of Danny Park. Not surprisingly, it was considered a 'secure location' for the prime minister, David Lloyd George, and members of the government to meet.

The owner, Colonel W. H. Campion, at that time fighting in Belgium, rented his home to Lord (then Sir George) Riddell for the summer and autumn of 1918. Although unaware of the exact purpose of the let, he stipulated that a visitors' book should be kept recording the many government visitors to Danny from 30th June to 13th October 1918.

Like most country houses in this part of Sussex, Danny faces east because 'the south wind doth corrupt and make evyl vapours', according to a medical book of the time. The present house, built in 1595 in an 'E' shape in honour of Queen Elizabeth I, has many typically Elizabethan features, with two of the three wings remaining virtually unaltered ever since.

The Great Hall, completed in 1595, is 45ft long by 25ft high. Family portraits and heirlooms of the Campions, owners of Danny from 1725 to 1983, are on display, together with portraits of King Charles I, King Louis VIII of France and Queen Anne, and an 18th century fireback in the Great Hall showing Neptune driving his horses into the sea. However, the centuries old family letters dating from 1728 once displayed in the Great Hall are now housed in the library.

Drafts of the Armistice talks were formulated in stages over several months with many notable visitors: Sir Maurice (later Lord) Hankey, secretary to the Cabinet; Winston Churchill, minister of munitions; Admiral Sir Rosslyn Wemyss; and Lord Reading, First Sea Lord and Commander, Imperial General Staff. Later, Lord Reading was the ambassador in Washington on a special mission to President Wilson.

During the six months Lloyd George rented Danny, his wife Margaret, his daughter Megan and his secretary/mistress Frances Stevenson all spent time at the house. Intriguingly, the visitors' book dated 14th July 1918 and 13th October 1918 reveals that both women were present on the same day.

Lloyd George, with a reputation as a womanizer, continued his affair throughout. In A.J.P. Taylor's book *My Darling Pussy* one of his letters written from Danny during this period confirms his strong feelings towards Frances: 'My darling pussy, You might phone from the Treasury on Friday if you can come. Don't let Hankey see you. If Saturday impossible, what about Monday? Fondest love to my own. D.'

Another letter dated 5th October 1918, surely written tongue in cheek, reads: 'This is not a love-letter – it is a purely business communication or rather a minute from a Chief to his Secretary . . .'

Clearly, it was not all work and no play. Wolstonbury Hill, under which the house stands, was another diversion, as Lloyd George's close friend Lord Riddell recorded in his war diary on 13th and 14th July 1918: 'In the afternoon the PM, Borden [Sir Robert, PM of Canada] and [Field-Marshal, then General]

Danny and Wolstonbury Hill.

Smuts climbed (Wolstonbury) Hill. The PM and Borden returned covered in perspiration and forthwith had to bathe.'

The dining room overlooking the tranquil formal gardens and park, and the well stocked, wood panelled library, full of morocco-bound volumes, provided Lloyd George with welcome distraction, observed Lord Riddell: '20 and 21 July. Danny again. LG at work with his legs cocked up in the window seat of the dining room . . . He gets down from the Library shelves Bright's Speeches: quotes Byron's letters, which he has read habitually: Macaulay's Essays.'

Some weeks later, on 29th September 1918, the terms of the Armistice to be granted to Bulgaria were decided and were signed in the White Bedroom, overlooking Wolstonbury, where Lloyd George was confined to bed. On the same day, Sir Eric Geddes left for a meeting with President Wilson in America to discuss the general terms for which an armistice might be granted to Germany.

When Riddell visited on 13th October, the last day at Danny, matters were coming to a head. It was extremely busy with lunch, conferences and members of the War Cabinet who '. . . set to work to write memoranda expressing the decisions arrived at, each in a separate room . . .'

Sir Maurice Hankey adds: 'Arriving at 2.30 I found the PM, Bonar Law, Balfour, Churchill, Lord Reading, First Sea Lord, CIGS [Chief of the Imperial General Staff], with Philip Kerr [Lloyd George's private secretary]. We conferred for three hours on the subject of the German acceptance of President Wilson's conditions. . . . And a telegram was sent to him.'

This was from the magnificent Great Hall on 13th October 1918, when a cable was sent to President Wilson authorising him to go ahead with negotiations for an armistice with Germany. The panel on the west wall of the Great Hall commemorates this historic date. On 11th November Admiral Wemyss and the Allied Commander Marshal Ferdinand Foch met the German delegation, led by Major-General Detlef von Winterfeldt, in a railway carriage in Compiegne, France and the Armistice was signed, bringing the Great War to an end.

Over the years, Danny has had many roles. In World War I the house was used as a hospital for the British sick and wounded. From 1939 to 1945 it was the headquarters for officers of the Canadian and British armies, with the fields surrounding the house full of amphibious vehicles waiting to cross the Channel prior to the Normandy invasion.

Situated near Brighton, Glyndebourne and the Plumpton racecourses, Danny has attracted many illustrious visitors, including Queen Mary, King Edward VII, prime ministers and government officials who have enjoyed the beauty of Danny Park and the quiet elegance of the house.

Today, the house is privately owned by Mr and Mrs Richard Burrows, who provide residential apartments for the retired. A keen historian, Mr Burrows is interested in restoration and preservation of the Great Hall, library and rooms containing portraits, heirlooms and the visitors' book with the signatures of government ministers, Lloyd George, his wife and daughter and, on a lighter note, the paw mark of Lloyd George's dog Guizo.

Although Danny is no longer open to the public, Richard Burrows is happy to consider visits by appointment to a house where today's visitor can saviour the peace and tranquillity of the Sussex countryside and imagine Lloyd George walking over Wolstonbury Hill with his dog so many years ago.

Fact File:

Danny House, Hurstpierpoint, Hassocks, Sussex, BN6 9BB. Tel: 01273 833000. Location: Between Hassocks and Hurstpierpoint (B2116) off New Way Lane, one mile from Hassocks Station.

The Brighton Pylons, the Duke and Duchess of York and Sir Herbert Carden

'Hail guest, we ask not what thou art. If friend we greet thee hand and heart. If stranger such no longer be. If foe our love shall conquer thee.'

This is the inscription on the western pylon, one of the twin stone gate pillars on the A23 designed by Brighton architect John Denman as a welcome to those travelling into Brighton and for locals returning home.

The gates mark the northern limit of 'Greater Brighton', which was created on 1st April 1928. The climax was on 30th May 1928, when, at the invitation of Brighton Corporation, the Duke and Duchess of York (later King George VI and Queen Elizabeth) laid the foundation stones in front of a cheering crowd lining the four miles from Brighton.

'A Right Royal Day' was the headline in the *Sussex Daily News* of 31st May 1928. Beside the western pylon, there was a temporary dais 'carpeted, seated and decorated' in preparation for the ceremony, with more seats provided for VIPs from the council. The road was closed for all traffic and 'in the spacious roadway was drawn up a Royal guard of the Sussex R.N.V.R.'

The newspaper described the occasion in glowing terms: 'The ceremony at the pylons, the chief event of the day, was impressive without being heavily

Brighton Pylons, looking north.

pompous, and the speech of welcome delivered by the Mayor (Alderman Charles Kingston, J.P.) was a model of what such an address should be.'

The mayor presented VIPs, including Alderman Herbert Carden, to the royal couple. This was followed by speeches and then the ceremony itself. Using a broad mallet for the western pylon's foundation stone, the Duchess of York 'tapped it thrice and declared it "well and truly laid"'. The Duke and dignitaries crossed the road, where the Duke laid the foundation stone for the eastern pylon before returning to the dais for a prayer blessing 'this town', the Lord's Prayer and the National Anthem.

The cost of erecting the three-sided stone pylons was borne by public subscriptions amounting to £900 and a generous contribution of £2,545 from the wealthy socialist solicitor Sir Herbert Carden. A dedicated Brighton councillor and alderman, who served on the council from 1895 until his death in 1941, he was knighted for his work and affectionately known as 'the father of modern Brighton'. He served as mayor on several occasions, during which time he bought large tracts of land to sell back to the corporation at cost price, thereby protecting it from the developers.

The builders Field and Cox erected the pylons using Clipsham stone. In the centre of the largest block of the western pylon is a specially made box containing silver and copper coins of 1928 and copies of the *Sussex Daily News* and *The Times*. Also placed in the box for posterity were a history of the building of the pylons, a leather book with the names of the subscribers and their subscriptions ranging from 2s. 6d to £100 and a council diary of that year.

Originally, the pylons flanked a single-track road, then known as London Road, near Pyecombe. However, when the A23 was upgraded and widened in the early 1990s, the name BRIGHTON was added to the eastern pylon and both were cleaned and refurbished at considerable cost. Later on there was some controversy when it was suggested that one of the pillars should be demolished, but a public outcry ensued and the idea was quickly dropped.

Since then, there have been suggestions to build a third pylon as a tribute to Sir Herbert Carden's outstanding contribution to the city and to restore the

symmetry to Brighton's gateway. Nothing has come of it yet, but so many years after the historic ceremony in May 1928, the pylons remain one of the most iconic symbols of Brighton.

The eastern pylon.

G.K. Chesterton, Ditchling and Father Brown

Gilbert Keith Chesterton, better known as G.K. Chesterton, is considered one of the finest writers of the 20th century. He was born on 29th May 1874 in Campden Hill, London, and educated at St Paul's, London, but unlike many of his friends he never went to Oxford University. Instead he attended the Slade School of Art before becoming a journalist, scholar, novelist, writer, poet and cartoonist, with strong links to the village of Ditchling under the South Downs.

His many friends and associates in Ditchling included Hilary Pepler, printer, writer and poet, and the great artist-craftsman, Eric Gill, of Sopers in Ditchling High Street, together the founders in 1920 of the Catholic community of craftsmen on Ditchling Common, The Guild of St Joseph and St Dominic. The calligrapher Edward Johnston also admired his work greatly. According to his daughter Priscilla Johnston, in her biography *Edward Johnston*, he read *The Innocence of Father Brown* nineteen times methodically, entering the dates upon the flyleaf on each occasion.

A prolific writer, he wrote a hundred books, hundreds of poems, five plays, five novels and two hundred short stories. He also contributed to the *Daily News* and wrote a weekly column for *The Illustrated London News* from 1905 until his death thirty-one years later. However, he is probably best remembered for his popular series and best known character, the priest-detective Father Brown, based on Monsignor John O'Connor and second only to Sherlock Holmes in popularity during the 1900s. His other great work was 'The Ballad of the White Horse', also published in 1911.

At 6ft 4in and around 21 stone, Chesterton favoured a large broad-brimmed hat, a voluminous cloak and a walking stick. A cigar in his mouth, a walrus moustache and a small pair of glasses on the end of his nose completed the picture. He was sociable and affable, counting H.G. Wells, Max Beerbohm and the slim, angular George Bernard Shaw amongst his friends.

On one occasion, the humorous and quick-witted Chesterton remarked to his friend: 'To look at you, anyone would think there was a famine in England,' to which the equally quick-witted Shaw replied: 'To look at you, anyone would think you caused it.'

In 1900 Chesterton met Hilaire Belloc, an influential and lifelong friend with whom he worked on several books, using his cartoon skills acquired from the Slade School of Art. A year later he married the love of his life, Frances

Blogg. Frances remained a great influence throughout their marriage, attending to all aspects of his busy schedule assisted by their devoted secretary Dorothy Collins, whom the Chestertons treated as the surrogate child they never had.

When the famously absent-minded Chesterton missed a train, he sent his wife a telegram: 'Am at Market Harborough. Where ought I to be?' 'Home,' was her prompt reply. On another occasion, Chesterton and his wife were at Paddington station in 1909 when, purely by chance, they decided to take the next departing train. This happened to be for Slough, where they disembarked to walk to Beaconsfield – and, liking what they saw, they made it their home for the rest of their lives.

In the 1930s Chesterton's connections with mid Sussex remained strong. According to Janet Cragg of Ditchling Museum, he is believed to have visited Gerard Meynell in Ditchling, founder of Westminster Press and printers of *G.K's Weekly*. He was also a regular contributor to the Ditchling Press, like his father before him, and a frequent visitor to the general village store and delicatessen at the crossroads, now known as Chesterton's. Following one of his visits, he wrote the poem 'The Song Against Grocers'.

A deeply religious man defending Christianity and the Catholic Faith, he converted to Catholicism in 1922, preaching as a lay preacher at the Unitarian

The Old Meeting House in Ditchling, where Chesterton preached.

Church in the Twitten, Ditchling (now the Old Meeting House), where a larger than average chair was provided for Chesterton's larger than average physique!

Never short of an opinion, he was not afraid to stand up for what he believed. He opposed socialism, communism and capitalism or, as he saw it, the concentration of wealth for a small minority at the expense of the majority. Chesterton favoured 'distributism', the wider distribution of personal property throughout society by means of devising schemes and where necessary, legislation to enable small family businesses and farms to survive in a modern economy.

He took a considerable interest in the distributist community in Ditchling, which included Eric Gill and the Dominican Friar Vincent McNabb, but this petered out in 1936.

Chesterton was known throughout England as a result of the paper, *The EyeWitness* from 1911–12 edited by Hilaire Belloc and his brother Cecil Chesterton until Cecil joined the Army in 1916. *The EyeWitness* then became *The New Witness*, from 1912–23 edited by Chesterton himself before becoming *G.K.'s Weekly* from 1925–36, advocating distributism. Contributors included Belloc, Shaw, H.G. Wells and, on a regular basis, Eric Gill. When Chesterton died in 1936 it became *The Weekly Review*.

Many writers admired his work, among them Agatha Christie, Graham Greene, Evelyn Waugh, Ernest Hemingway, Kingsley Amis and Dorothy L. Sayers. He was also warmly received on the two occasions he visited America. Today his popularity continues and The American Chesterton Society in Minneapolis is dedicated to keeping his memory alive. His many trips included his three-month visit to Italy accompanied by his wife Frances and, as always, the faithful Dorothy where he interviewed Mussolini and had an audience with Pope Pius XI.

Chesterton died on June 14th, 1936 at his home in Beaconsfield, Buckinghamshire. He is buried in the Catholic Cemetery in Shepherd's Lane, Beaconsfield, and the monument over his grave is the work of Eric Gill. Two years later, when his beloved wife Frances died, she was buried beside him. Dorothy Collins lived close by until her death in 1988 when she was buried beside them.

Fact File:

Ditchling is north of Brighton under Ditchling Beacon.

The Kipling Room – By kind permission of The Grange Museum and Art Gallery, Rottingdean.

Rudyard Kipling,
Literary Giant of Sussex

Rudyard Kipling, the foremost writer of his time and creator of *The Jungle Book* and the *Just So Stories,* countless poems, short stories and novels, had a passion for Sussex, his home from 1897 until his death in 1936.

Born in India in 1865 to English parents, he was educated in England like many children of his background at the time. As an adult – slight, just 5ft 6in, balding and short-sighted with a strong cleft chin and a moustache – he developed a glittering international writing career in Lahore, South Africa and Vermont where he spent the first four years of his marriage.

In 1887, after a family rift with his brother-in-law, he left Vermont for England to settle in Rottingdean on the Sussex coast with his American wife Caroline Balestier – Carrie, then pregnant with their son John – and their two young daughters, Josephine and Elsie.

For three guineas a week, he rented The Elms, a 'marine residence' overlooking the Green at Rottingdean. Kipling knew the village well. Over the years, he had often stayed with Georgiana – Aunt Georgie – and her husband, the painter Edward Burne-Jones in North End House nearby. In addition to the Burne-Jones family, his cousin, the future prime minister Stanley Baldwin, had married Lucy, the eldest daughter of the Ridsdales who lived in the Dene by the Green.

In his autobiography, *Something of Myself,* Kipling described the close proximity of the Dene, North End House and the Elms where 'One could throw a cricket-ball from any one house to the other.' He also described 'packing farm-carts filled with mixed babies – Stanley Baldwin's and ours – and despatching them into the safe clean heart of the motherly Downs for jam-smeared picnics. Those Downs moved me to write some verses called 'Sussex'.'

'Sussex' became the unofficial anthem of the county. Other great works such as *Kim, Stalky and Co.,* the *Just So Stories* and his poems 'Recessional' and 'The Absent-Minded Beggar' were written at the Elms, where the chalk cliffs and the peace of Rottingdean inspired him.

A family man, he was delighted when his children went swimming using 'Trunky' Thomas's bathing machine or fishing off Magnus Volk's outlandish contraption, the 'Pioneer', the stilted passenger carriage of the 'Daddy-Long-Legs' railway moored at the pier head off Rottingdean. He was also a 'maniac' motorist, venturing into the Sussex countryside in 'his very own' locomobile, nick-named the Holy Terror or Coughing Jane, driven by his chauffeur and the inspiration for 'Steam Tactics', written in 1902.

The Kiplings enjoyed an enviable lifestyle spending the winter months in warmer climates. In 1898, the family spent four months in Cape Province, South Africa in The Woolsack, the Dutch colonial home given to them by Cecil Rhodes. In 1899, they set off once again, taking Carrie, Josephine and Elsie on a trip to America. After a rough crossing, tragedy struck in New York when Kipling and his eldest daughter Josephine, contracted pneumonia. Kipling pulled through but Josephine, aged just six died, leaving her parents bereft.

Josephine, Kipling's fair-haired 'little American' and the 'best beloved' child, was the apple of her father's eye. After her death, Elsie, his younger daughter wrote later: 'A light had gone out that could never be rekindled.'

On their return to Rottingdean, Kipling was haunted by Josephine's spirit all around him. This, and the local publican of the White Horse running double-decker horse buses packed with Brighton trippers hoping to glimpse their hero in his garden, was the last straw.

Carrie began house hunting, wisely abandoning the Holy Terror, their unreliable American steam-driven locomobile to take a train to Etchingham and a 'fly' – a horse drawn carriage – to view Bateman's in Burwash, East Sussex. On entering the house, Kipling 'felt her spirit – her Feng Shui – to be good'. However, the owner had just let it, and they were obliged to wait until the tenancy was up before buying it for £9,300.

On 2nd September 1902, Carrie, Elsie and John moved to Bateman's and Kipling joined them the next day. The Jacobean house in the Dudwell Valley was built in 1634. It was inaccessible, prone to flooding and lacked modern facilities such as a bathroom, running water upstairs or electricity but it was exactly what Kipling wanted – 'a good and peaceable place'.

Kipling's financial rewards were the equivalent of J.K. Rowling's today, enabling him to set about improving his new home and the 33 acres that came with the property. The mill was converted to supply electricity to light the house with the aid of Sir William Willcocks who had installed the first Aswan Dam, a feat Kipling dismissed in comical comparison as 'a trifling affair on the Nile'. Other improvements were converting the two oast houses once used for hop and beer brewing into staff accommodation.

After his experiences in Rottingdean, Kipling was keener than ever to pre-serve his privacy, eventually acquiring more than 300 acres through 14 sepa-rate conveyances. Carrie's office had a porthole overlooking the hall, enabling her to monitor visitors to the house. There was no telephone, as Kipling preferred to send urgent messages by telegram or telephone from the Burwash post office. He burned his old papers in the stone fireplace, much to the dismay of his friend and American publisher Frank Doubleday. But Kipling was intensely private, declaring: 'No one's going to make a monkey out of me after I die.'

Over the years, the Kiplings had many influential friends for lunch and tea, others for overnight stays: A.P. Watt, Kipling's literary agent for 40 years; Frank Doubleday, his publisher; Max Aitken who later became Lord Beaverbrook; and VIPs from the Empire and the dominions. Children, the very elderly and the Kiplings' extended families all enjoyed their hospitality, if not their stiff, old-fashioned furniture and Spartan atmosphere.

Carrie kept at bay intrusive members of the press, the middle-aged whom they considered dull and the county set, earning her the dislike of many people. Nevertheless, she was ever protective and totally loyal towards her husband, acting as the buffer between him and the outside world.

In the mornings, from his book-lined study, Kipling would 'hatch' his stories on his table littered with crumpled up blue sheets of paper and discarded drafts of work. Surrounded by souvenirs from the Far East, and covered in black ink-stains from his hand-dipped Waverley pen, he would pace up and down humming to himself before retiring to his hard day-bed to 'wait for my Daemon' (his sub-conscious) to strike.

Lunch at one o'clock would follow, often with friends or relatives, his sister Trish, the Baldwins, the Burne-Jones, cousins, aunts and uncles, and Kipling's much loved Aberdeen terriers very much in evidence.

The Weald and Bateman's inspired him to write many works on the Sussex countryside, using the books on the county in his library and the wonderful views all around him. *Puck of Pook's Hill*, written primarily for his own children Elsie and John, appealed to readers around the world and *Rewards and Fairies* was another great success.

In 1907 Kipling was invited to Stockholm, where he became the first Englishman to receive the Nobel Prize for Literature. The prize money of seven thousand guineas was spent installing a shallow, rectangular water pond, a rose garden, a yew hedge with a circular wooden seat and a sundial facing south. In the visitors' book Kipling entered the names of those who fell into the pond with FIP beside them – Fell into Pond! Others who outstayed their welcome found themselves standing in front of the sundial reading the inscription: 'It is later than you think.'

From Bateman's he continued motoring and touring Sussex, describing the car as a 'time-machine on which one can slide from one century to another at no more than the pushing forward of a lever'. He also delighted in watching his Aberdeen terriers taking biscuits from the chairs around the room, including those of his stuffier guests. His Guernsey cows, kept for appearance rather than profit, were given names such as Bateman's Blizzard and Bateman's Baby, while Kipling pets were lovingly given their own graves at the bottom of the garden.

Despite the loss of Josephine some years earlier, Kipling had found happiness at Bateman's, working hard and enjoying the company of Carrie, Elsie and John, his farming interests and the stream of influential friends and visitors.

Sadly, this happiness was shattered when World War One broke out. All the young men were enlisting and Kipling, known as the Poet of the Empire and counting King George V and the prime minister amongst his circle, wanted his son to fight the 'Hun', as did John himself.

He was profoundly short-sighted like his father and was rejected by the army and navy as 'a danger to himself and to his men'. Kipling ignored their views. Instead, he persuaded his friend Field Marshal Lord Roberts to arrange a commission for John in the Irish Guards in the summer of 1915.

Newly commissioned, John returned to Bateman's before leaving for France. On 17th August 1915, his mother recorded proudly in her diary: 'He looks very straight and smart and young and brave as he turns at the top of the stairs to say, "Send my love to Daddo".'

On 27th September 1915, in pouring rain, Second Lieutenant John Kipling was killed in the Battle of Loos on the first day of action. He was just 18.

Grieving and filled with guilt, Kipling refused to accept that John had died, desperately hoping that he was just 'missing'. He made every effort to find out

Bateman's. The author's study is on the first floor on the left.

what had become of him, calling on influential friends including the Prince of Wales to obtain news, but to no avail. Not surprisingly, he became introspective, developing duodenal ulcers that were treated without success by his doctor.

Afterwards he wrote bitterly: 'If any question why we died/ Tell them, because our fathers lied.' He also wrote the haunting poem 'My Boy Jack', famous for the line: 'Have you news of my boy Jack?'

When the war ended, Kipling became an active commissioner for Sir Fabian Ware's Imperial War Graves Commission, the group responsible for creating British war graves in Europe and other locations around the world. He also supported the creation of the Tomb of the Unknown Soldier at Westminster Abbey.

Tireless in his support of the families who had lost loved ones, he visited military cemeteries on the former Western Front, accompanied by Carrie and King George V. At home, he attended the unveiling of the white dome of the Chattri on the Sussex Downs in 1921, and two years later, his two-volume history of the Irish Guards – his son's regiment – was published.

When Elsie, the Kipling's one surviving child, left to marry George Bambridge in 1924, Bateman's seemed empty and overwhelming. Bravely, Kipling ignored his ill-health and enormous personal losses to write *Debits and Credits* in 1926, *Limits and Renewals* in 1932 and *Something of Myself* published posthumously in 1937.

At Bateman's the flow of guests continued unabated. In 1933, 140 people came to lunch or tea, each name faithfully entered in the visitors' book by Kipling himself, rather than his guests. Yet he remained modest and shy by nature, declining many honours, including a knighthood, the poet laureateship and the order of merit.

In January 1936, three days before his King, Kipling died of peritonitis when the gastric ulcer that had plagued him since 1915 haemorrhaged whilst on a visit to London with Carrie. He was just 70.

After a secret cremation at Golders Green, his ashes were interred at Poet's Corner in Westminster on 23rd January 1936. Carrie battled on at Bateman's until her death three years later, when her ashes were placed under a tree in the walled garden. With no grandchildren, Carrie left Bateman's and its contents to the National Trust as a memorial to her husband's long and extraordinary career.

Fact File:

The Grange Museum and Art Gallery, Rottingdean. Tel: 01273 296918
Bateman's, Burwash, East Sussex, TN19 7DS. Tel: 01435 882302

All aboard Volk's Electric Railway!

Hassocks Inventor Magnus Volk and his Electric Railway

For many, Magnus Volk is remembered as the inventor of the first electric railway in the British Isles, which opened on August 4th 1883 in Brighton. It is the oldest passenger-carrying narrow gauge electric railway in the world, running from the Aquarium down to Black Rock.

A resident of Hassocks from 1903 to 1914, Magnus Volk enjoyed the peace and tranquillity of the countryside while commuting to Brighton to continue his work on his brainchild, Volk's Electric Railway.

Born on 19th October 1851 at 40 Western Road, Brighton, Magnus Volk was the son of a German clockmaker. At an early age he showed a keen interest in anything mechanical and 'how it worked', earning him the nickname 'Magnus the dreamer'. In 1869, at the age of 17, his clockmaker father died, leaving him to successfully run the family business.

While still only in his twenties, he employed more than a dozen people and made a simple telegraph set which sold all over the world. He continued experimenting with telegraphy, telephony and electricity and his 'parlour telegraph' became popular. Magnus was dedicated to 'the electricity', still in its infancy. In 1879, when he married Anna Banfield, the second daughter of a Baptist family of six girls and three boys, he proudly entered 'electrician' as his profession on the marriage certificate.

With his keen interest in all things electrical, it is not surprising that in 1880 the ever-inventive Magnus equipped his house in Brighton with the first telephone and electric light system, a considerable achievement all those years ago.

Suitably impressed, Brighton Corporation gave him the contract for installing the electric incandescent lighting in the Royal Pavilion, which he completed in 1883 – the year he also opened Volk's Railway to the public for the first time.

As Brighton was a town of horse-drawn carriages, it was a great novelty for passengers to board Volk's Electric Train at the main entrance to the Aquarium (now the Sea life Centre). Their trip ended approximately a quarter of a mile to the east at the Old Chain Pier, later destroyed by gales and furious seas in 1886. Nowadays passengers board the train at the Aquarium Station, either alighting at Peter Pan's Playground Station, the midway point, or continuing to Black Rock Marina Station, or vice versa.

Another famous invention was Magnus Volk's 'Daddy-Long-Legs' (alias 'Pioneer'). Advertised as 'A Sea Voyage on Wheels, in Brighton – Fare 6d Each Way', the strange 40-ton saloon car ran on 24ft-high stilts along an ultra-wide track dug deep into the chalk seabed approximately halfway between the high and low water mark.

The inaugural run took place on 29th November 1896 but, sadly, the sea destroyed the outlandish-looking contraption just a few days later. However, with his usual determination, Magnus quickly repaired it and on Sunday, February 20th, 1898, the Prince of Wales, later Edward VII, and the Duke and Duchess of Fife enjoyed two pleasure trips aboard the saloon car, reminiscent of a tramcar, yacht and seaside pier all rolled into one.

In 1903, Magnus, his wife Anna and three of their seven children moved from their poky house in Clermont Terrace, Brighton to Hassocks, just seven miles north of his workshop under the cliffs. The couple leased Hassocks Farm House near Stanford Avenue and London Road, and Magnus continued walking, driving and cycling in the Weald under the South Downs while searching for a suitable home to buy.

Conrad Volk's book *Magnus Volk of Brighton* describes how his parents loved exploring the countryside in a pony and trap rented from the farmer, either with their three children or alone. During this time, the couple attended

The railway running along Madeira Drive.

the Hassocks Congregational Church (now the United Reformed Church) where Magnus helped to find an organ for the church's use indefinitely.

In 1906 Magnus bought Shelburne, a three-story semi-detached house in Chancellors Park, where the family lived in comfort with a nanny and maids to look after them. Always community spirited and with a love of children, Magnus allowed the meadow belonging to Shelburne to be made available for treats, fetes and other village get-togethers. He also delighted in playing Father Christmas, when he would appear on friends' doorsteps with presents for their children.

Apart from his work on the railways and the installation of the first electric lighting in the Brighton Royal Pavilion, Magnus Volk's inventions were very diverse. In 1881 he was awarded a gold medal for his fire alarm system. He equipped Brighton's telephone exchange, and in 1887 he constructed an electric dogcart, which the Sultan of Constantinople promptly ordered. An inveterate traveller, Magnus wasted no time in delivering and demonstrating the cart in the palace grounds himself. His inventiveness was boundless, and in World War I, he installed X-ray equipment in a Brighton hospital, designed an egg-cup for one-armed soldiers and much more.

On 4th August 1933 Volk's Railway became the first railway in the world to celebrate 50 years of service. However, with the outbreak of World War II and the government's decision to close all beaches, it was forced to shut down for defence work to be carried out. After the war, the track was renewed from end to end, and from May 1948 it was 'business as usual' once again.

Today, Volk's Electric Railway, designed and built by Magnus Volk in just three to six weeks, continues to carry up to eighty passengers along the Brighton seafront. Over the years celebrities such as Anna Neagle, Robert Morley, Dora Bryan and Julian Clary have been among the many thousands of passengers to have enjoyed a ride on the little railway on the front built more than one-and-a-quarter centuries ago.

Magnus Volk died at the age of 84 a day after attending the opening of the new redesigned Black Rock Station on 7th May 1937. His final wish was granted when he was buried in the churchyard at Ovingdean, Brighton, near the Sussex Downs he knew and loved throughout his life.

Fact File:

**Volk's Electric Railway, Madeira Drive, Brighton, BN2 1EN.
Tel: 01273 292718.**

Replicas of John Logie Baird's television apparatus and 'Stookie Bill' – By kind permission of Hastings Museum and Art Gallery. (See page 69.)

John Logie Baird, Television Pioneer of Hastings

In 1924, John Logie Baird, the inventor of the first electro-mechanical television system, made history when he transmitted the very first moving picture – the Maltese Cross of a St John Ambulance Medal – from his laboratory in Hastings.

A mild-mannered Scot, he was born on the 13th August 1888 at The Lodge, 121 West Argyle Street, Helensburgh in Dunbartonshire. However, his health was not good, and he suffered from bronchial problems that continued throughout his life, eventually causing him to move to Hastings in 1923.

He was the youngest of four children, his parents being the Rev John Baird and his wife Jessie Morrison Inglis. Educated at Larchfield Academy, he showed a keen and inventive interest in how things worked. By the age of 13 he had made a generator to install electricity in the family home, had designed a remote control for a camera and had constructed a glider. His son Malcolm recalls how his father rigged up a telephone network using a wooden box no bigger than a shoebox in his bedroom to communicate with his friends living on the opposite side of the street. His other interest – television - shaped his adult life.

After school he attended the Glasgow and West of Scotland Technical College where he studied electrical engineering, receiving an associateship from the college in 1914. He attended the University of Glasgow as a final year BSc degree student, but his studies were disrupted by the outbreak of World War One and he never graduated.

From 1916 he worked for the Clyde Valley Electrical Power Company as an assistant mains engineer. With the war raging, he was keen to enlist, but his health let him down and he was pronounced unfit for medical service. He continued working for the company until his resignation in 1918, when he turned to a series of business ventures with limited financial success.

Looking like a typical inventor with a mane of thick hair and glasses, he had a diverse career which included spells in Glasgow, the West Indies and London, where he marketed a variety of products including fertilizer and coir fibre, boot polish and medicated, thermal socks – the Baird Undersock – which he sold from door to door.

His next venture was in Trinidad, where he marketed jam until he contracted malaria. He returned to England where he sold mango chutney and guava jelly stock to a sausage maker for £15 before trying his hand at selling industrial soap cleaners in London. But his health continued to cause concern and he left the city on doctor's orders for the bracing fresh air of the Sussex coast.

From February 1923 to November 1924, he retired to Hastings virtually penniless to share lodgings with his old Glaswegian friend Guy Robertson, known as 'Mephy' at 21 Linton Crescent, Hastings.

He remained interested in television, and financed his own research using the simplest and cheapest means of resolving technical problems, often assisted by the Hastings, St Leonards and District Radio Society.

From Linton Crescent, he used a bull's-eye lense, a tea chest, a biscuit-tin and a toy electric motor to construct his first successful television prototype. Later on he added more lenses and a 'Nipkow disc' used for scanning pictures in narrow parallel lines. Initially he produced a faint but identifiable 'shadow-graph' of a cardboard cross. This was later replaced when that first flickering image of a Maltese Cross was transmitted on a tiny screen in January 1924. The historical occasion witnessed by journalists from the *Daily News* and the *Hastings Observer* generated great interest from the public, and more demonstrations followed.

His second laboratory in Hastings was over a shop in Queens Arcade, where he studied the development of television and how to transmit and receive visual signals from a laboratory. However, not all his experiments went smoothly. On one occasion he was flung across his laboratory, when he electrocuted himself with a thousand volts – much to the concern of his landlord, Alderman Ben Went Tree. A fascinated crowd watched as Baird stood on the pavement in split trousers (the result of the experiment that went wrong), arguing with Tree, who ordered him to leave Queen's Arcade.

Eventually letters from Tree's solicitors persuaded Baird to vacate the premises in favour of London, where he continued his work on image transmission. On 25th March 1925 he demonstrated his mechanical system at Selfridges Store by sending a recognisable but weak picture signal of moving silhouette images a short distance. Some months later, on 2nd October 1925, he transmitted the first television picture of the head of a ventriloquist's dummy he called 'Stooky Bill' (a Scottish word meaning 'plaster') from his workshop in Frith Street, Soho. Elated, Baird rushed downstairs to repeat the experiment on William Taynton, a 20-year-old office boy, who became the first human face ever to be televised in full tonal range.

He formed his first television company and, with financial backing, created Baird Television Development Company (BTDC) in 1927. In the same year, in front of forty members of the Royal Institution in London, he gave a formal demonstration of an image of a moving object using his 30-line television system, the first of its kind in the world. The demonstration was a great success and subsequently, France, Germany, America and other parts of the world adopted his system.

At the invitation of Hastings and District Radio Society he returned to Hastings in 1927 to lecture at the White Rock Pavilion. In 1928 his company, successfully transmitted the first trans-Atlantic images of the faces of people being interviewed between London and New York. Other achievements in the same year were demonstrating colour television, stereoscopic television and the first transmission to a ship – the Berengaria – in mid Atlantic.

A master of improvisation, brimming with ideas that he often jotted down on tablecloths and napkins at restaurants, Baird was at the peak of his success. In 1929 Hastings honoured him when the mayor, Cllr Thorpe, invited him to the unveiling ceremony of a commemorative plaque in Queens Arcade, the location of his old laboratory.

Abroad, the German post office backed him in 1929 and commissioned a TV service, but in Britain the reaction was very different. Sir John Reith, the autocratic first director general of the BBC, described Baird's television as: 'A potential social menace of the first magnitude!' However, after pressure from the British post office, they lent him studio facilities for his experiments and broadcast the first sound and vision telecast in 1930 using his 30-line system. Baird's system, however, was unable to produce images bigger than 9 inches by 4 inches, and by 1935 the BBC selected the all-electric TV system of his rival Marconi, and Baird's was dropped two years later.

The 1930s were a busy time for Baird. He televised the Derby twice, demonstrated cinema television in black and white and colour and, in 1931, married a South African pianist, Margaret Albu, in New York. They had two children, Diana and Malcolm.

Another project was 'Noctovision', a system by which objects are viewed in complete darkness using infra-red rays transmitted to an ordinary receiver. A canny Scot, Baird took out more than 170 patents to protect his inventions. In addition to this, he frequently took key components home with him at night and concealed the true progress of his discoveries by allowing the press access only to research achieved a few stages earlier.

In 1941 he returned to Sussex, where he lived at Station Road, Bexhill, with his wife and two children. His ill health and financial worries continued yet, despite this, he successfully televised the post-war victory parade in June 1946. Just days later he died peacefully in his sleep, on 14th June 1946, aged 57.

Sadly Baird, the forerunner of television as we know it today, died in near poverty. His companies became outmoded and unable to compete with new, more sophisticated systems, such as Marconi-EMI, and his wish to achieve financial success for himself and his much loved family eluded him to the end.

Nevertheless, his amazing contribution to television was recognised in 1937 when Baird became the first Briton to receive the gold medal of the International Faculty of Science. And, in the words of Hastings Museum and Art Gallery, 'He was the first person to produce a live, moving television image of a remote scene illuminated by reflected light, reproduced in full tonal range.'

Baird could not have imagined his work would be the forerunner of world-wide television, progressing to other mediums such as videos and play-stations, to name just a few. Or that, on the other side of the world, major television awards in Australia would be named 'Logies' in his honour.

In the town where he carried out so many experiments, the Hastings Museum and Art Gallery has a superb exhibition of television history in which the burnt and singed face of 'Stooky Bill', a Baird 'televisor' and other artefacts can be seen.

Fact File:

Hastings Museum and Art Gallery, Bohemia Road, Hastings, East Sussex. Tel: 01424 451052.

'National Velvet' and Enid Bagnold of Rottingdean

'A wet and windy village full of rheumatism and beauty,' was writer Enid Bagnold's verdict regarding Rottingdean on the Sussex coast, her home from 1923 until her death in 1981.

Writing under her maiden name of Enid Bagnold, her most famous works are *National Velvet*, and the play *The Chalk Garden*. She was a passionate but often misunderstood woman, balancing her role as a wife, mother and grand society hostess with that of a writer and playwright known on both sides of the Atlantic.

Born in Rochester, Kent, in 1889, Enid was the daughter of an officer in the Royal Engineers. She spent a privileged childhood in Jamaica before returning to England, where she was educated at a progressive school in Godalming followed by finishing schools in Lausanne and Paris.

Independent, outspoken and bohemian, she studied art at Walter Sickert's School of Art in Chelsea where she met Henri Gaudier-Brzeska who sculpted her head in 1912. Soon afterwards, she left to pursue her main interest, becoming a journalist for *Hearth and Home* and *The Modern Society*.

The editor, Frank Harris was a 56-year-old womanizer past his prime, who described sex as 'the gateway to life'. Enid found him intriguing and enthralling, writing later: 'I went through the gateway in an upper room at the Café Royal.'

Frank Harris was 'the wonderful first to me' but not the last. When war broke out in 1914, she joined the Red Cross becoming a nurse at the Royal Herbert Hospital, London. Tall and striking in her starched apron and white uniform, she soon caught the eye of Romanian aristocrat Prince Antoine Bibesco, whom she loved with an unrequited passion for many years.

Critical of the hospital, and encouraged by Prince Antoine, she jotted down her observations as a nurse in her book *Diary Without Dates*. Within half an hour of the book's publication in 1918 she had been dismissed for a breach of military discipline. Undeterred by her dismissal, she volunteered to go to France to drive ambulances for the French army.

Diary Without Dates was her first literary success, with queues forming around the block to buy it. It was reviewed in the *Daily Mail* and described by H.G. Wells in *The Dream* (1924) as one of the most human books written about the war. She also used her experiences in France to write *The Happy Foreigner* (1920), a romance set against post-war France.

In 1920 she married Sir Roderick Jones, owner of Reuters News Agency. However, before she agreed to marry him, she struck a bargain: she would be the perfect society hostess in return for three uninterrupted hours every day for writing. Sir Roderick agreed and the marriage, officiated by the Archbishop of Cape Town, took place at Chelsea Old Church. The church was adorned with red roses and bay trees, and countless aristocrats and diplomats attended the reception.

In 1923, the Jones family moved to North End House, Rottingdean, originally two buildings named Prospect House and Aubrey Cottage, and previously the home of Sir Edward Burne-Jones, the painter. It was an imposing house overlooking the Green, with ample room for Enid to escape to the round tower room for her daily writing sessions.

Sir Roderick was incredibly wealthy, enabling him to extend North End House by buying the neighbouring Gothic House in 1927. Other properties he bought in Rottingdean were Rudyard Kipling's former home, the Elms, and Dale Cottage used as a racing stable.

Enid and Sir Roderick had three sons and a daughter. In 1930, Enid, a devoted mother with a great love of children, wrote *Alice and Thomas and*

North End House, Rottingdean.

Jane. Once again, she drew on her own life to write the adventures of three children – aged five, seven and eight – who lived in a large house in Rottingdean, very similar to her own family and circumstances.

Five years later *National Velvet* was published. Set in a fictitious village with a green and a pond like Rottingdean, the story is about Velvet Brown, a 14-year-old butcher's daughter who wins a piebald in a raffle. Velvet quickly discovers that her new horse is a natural jumper and, with gold sovereigns won by Velvet's mother when she was a young swimmer, enters him in the Grand National. Mi Taylor, the butcher's assistant, based on the Jones' groom Bernard McHardy, trains the horse – and Velvet, disguised as a boy, goes on to win the Grand National.

National Velvet was dedicated to, and partly inspired by, Enid's 13-year-old daughter Laurian who also drew several illustrations for the book. Enid included her own love of riding to portray Velvet, while Velvet's sisters were a combination based on the daughters of General Asquith (who rented the Elms from Sir Roderick) and the village butcher's daughters.

Rave reviews followed, and *National Velvet* was an instant success. However, in Rottingdean, the book – and Enid – received a cool reception. Villagers objected to the similarities between the fictitious Browns and the 'real-life' residents, the Hilders. Velvet's mother, Mrs Brown, was an excellent swimmer like Mrs Hilder. Velvet's father was the village butcher, like Mr Hilder, and Velvet and her sisters were too similar to the Hilder children. Mrs Hilder felt Enid's description of her was unflattering, but what rankled the most was that Enid chose to buy her meat from another butcher!

Enid's literary success and the Jones's immense wealth did not impress the villagers of Rottingdean. The family employed a cook, a butler, housemaids, a lady's maid, two nursery nurses, a chauffeur to drive the Rolls Royce, Buick and Dodge and a groom for the children's four horses. There were also sumptuous parties every weekend, when the maids related the 'goings-on' at North End House, fuelling village gossip.

The weekend parties were difficult for Enid who, whenever possible, escaped her guests to dig in the solitude of the fields. However, in 1953 she used her memories of the packed garden room to write *The Chalk Garden*, which was put on stage in London and New York. The play, with Edith Evans and Peggy Ashcroft in lead roles, opened in London in 1956. In America, Enid was awarded the silver medal of the American Academy of Arts and Letters. Ten years after the London production, *The Chalk Garden* was filmed starring Edith Evans, Deborah Kerr, Hayley Mills and John Mills.

The family divided their time between Rottingdean and their London home in Hyde Park Gate, yet Enid was devoid of snobbery. She was happy to mix with people from all backgrounds, including the staff's children as well as prominent writers and famous actresses such as Kathryn Hepburn and Elizabeth Taylor. In her book *Notable Sussex Women*, Helena Wojtczak describes Elizabeth Taylor visiting Lady Jones on several occasions. No doubt surprised Rottingdean locals would have enjoyed the 'star quality' the actress brought with her!

In 1944, when MGM made *National Velvet* into a film starring 12-year-old Elizabeth Taylor and Mickey Rooney, Enid received international acclaim. But her great passion remained the theatre, with North End House as the focal point for a varied social life, counting society photographer Cecil Beaton, Dame Anna Neagle, Charles Laughton, John Gielgud and Edith Evans amongst her friends.

Following her husband's death in 1962, Enid suffered from arthritis and sciatica. After a hip operation in 1969, when she was prescribed morphine to control the pain, she became addicted, injecting herself with up to 350mg of morphine a day for twelve years. Her health deteriorated, and she sold her London home in 1969 to return to 'wet and windy' Rottingdean. In an effort to become part of the village, she became patron of the Rottingdean Drama Society and president of the Rottingdean Preservation Society – yet she still remained the outsider.

Throughout her writing career she was a mother first, believing her children to be her greatest and most enduring memorial. Her writing was combined with

The Elms, Rottingdean.

a hectic family and social life, but in spite of this, she found time to write seven novels, nine plays, children's books, poetry and her autobiography, published in 1969.

In 1970, she was elected a Fellow of the Royal Society of Literature, and in 1976 she was awarded a CBE. There are commemorative plaques in London and Rottingdean, and Brighton bus 602 was named after her.

Aubrey House, Enid Bagnold's former home.

Today there is a renewed interest in her work, with a recent revival of her play *The Chalk Garden* at the Donmar Theatre in London. *National Velvet*, published by HarperCollins as a 'charming classic' is as popular as ever.

In her twilight years, she was determined to die at 17a Hamilton Terrace, London, where her father and grandfather had once lived. Her wish was granted on 31st March 1981, at the age of 92. She was cremated in Golders Green, and her ashes are buried in the family vault in St Margaret's parish churchyard, Rottingdean.

Fact File:

The Grange Museum and Art Gallery, Rottingdean: 01273 296918.

The Church of St John the Baptist, Clayton, where Norman Hartnell is buried.

Norman Hartnell,
By Royal Appointment

Sir Norman Bishop Hartnell was famous for his style, glamour and elegance, but perhaps most notably as the couturier to the Queen and the royal family for over 40 years.

Born on 12th June 1901 at 2 Streatham Hill, London, he was the only son of Henry Bishop Hartnell, a hotelier (and later Brighton councillor for Kingscliff Ward in the thirties) and Emma Mary Coulson, née Polley from the Hassocks area.

Norman and his sister Phyllis spent their early years in Honiton, Devon, before moving to Hassocks, where his grandmother lived at Southbank, near Stone Pound cross roads.

In his autobiography *Silver and Gold*, he describes himself as 'a sickly child forced to remain in bed for long periods . . . with a drawing block against my knees, weaving crude but fantastic designs'. His love of art continued both at home and at his school, Mill Hill, where he covered his exercise books with sketches of the actresses of the day.

On 3rd of April 1921 his beloved mother died aged 54. In the same year, Norman attended Magdalene College, Cambridge, to study architecture. He joined the Footlights Dramatic Club where he designed both the costumes and sets. After two years, and before obtaining his degree, he left university, following his father's refusal to support him for his third year at Cambridge, having lost money on the Stock Exchange. Later his father re-married, acquiring three stepdaughters, and the family settled in Brighton.

Norman obtained a job with Madame Desiree, the court dressmaker of 7 Hertford Street, W1, receiving £3 a week. However, in 1923 he and his sister Phyllis opened a couture establishment at 10 Bruton Street, London. His father paid the first year's rent while Norman established himself designing costumes for Gertrude Lawrence, playwrights Charles Cochran and Noel Coward and, in 1927 the wedding dress for Barbara Cartland.

Socialites Maud Messel of the famous Sussex family of Nymans, West Sussex and her daughter Anne, Countess of Rosse, the mother of Lord Snowdon wore Norman Hartnell evening dresses – the latter included in the Messel Exhibition held at Brighton Museum from October 2005 until July 2006.

A turning point came in 1935. He designed Lady Alice Montague-Douglas-Scott's wedding dress for her marriage to the Duke of Gloucester and the dresses for the bridesmaids, the young Princesses Elizabeth and Margaret. This led to the Duchess of York (later the Queen Mother) asking him to produce some designs for her, too.

In 1935 he moved to the more elegant premises of 26 Bruton Street, where he lived and worked, eventually employing 400 people and producing 2,000 gowns every year for his private customers and the royal family. He owned a country house, Lovel Dene in Windsor Forest, and the Tower House in Regent's Park.

In 1938, Hartnell was appointed official dressmaker to the British royal family, designing gowns for overseas visits and royal occasions, and in 1940 he received the royal warrant.

Across the pond, he made his name designing film costumes for more than 21 films. In 1947, he received the prestigious American Neiman-Marcus award for his exceptional contribution to fashion around the world. The Hartnell style became popular with many glamorous actresses of the day: Anna Neagle, Marlene Dietrich, Merle Oberon, Vivien Leigh, Tallulah Bankhead and Elizabeth Taylor, to name a few.

'To me, simplicity is the death of the soul,' he is famous for saying, having become renowned for his elaborately decorated gowns. Yet he was versatile and practical when needed. During World War II he was economic with fabric, buttons and other materials, designing 'utility' dresses for the mass market and ready-to-wear collections available through department stores. Hartnell also designed the uniforms for the British Red Cross, the Women's Royal Army Corps and the Women's Police Force.

In coronation year, he was awarded the MVO (Member of the Royal Victorian Order), while in 1977, after 40 years of designing for royalty, he was made a Knight Commander of the Victorian Order. He was the first couturier to be knighted, having designed state and evening dresses for Queen Mary, the Queen Mother and her daughter Queen Elizabeth II. In 1947 he designed the Queen's wedding dress containing 10,000 seed pearls and thousands of white crystal beads, and in 1953 her coronation gown.

A bachelor, he was popular, charming, debonair and witty, moving in theatrical circles and counting society photographer Cecil Beaton, playwright Noel Coward and socialite Bunny Roger amongst his close friends.

Despite poor health for the last 20 years of his life, he continued working diligently up until his death, at the age of 77, on 8th June 1979 at King Edward VII Hospital, Windsor.

On 15th June 1979, his funeral service took place at the Church of St John the Baptist, Clayton, near Ditchling. Keymer parish church choir led the singing and his old friend, the Rt Rev Mervyn Stockwood, Bishop of Southwark, and the rector of Clayton and Keymer, the Rev Ted Goodman, conducted the service.

Extra seating was arranged for his numerous friends, models and members of his staff who drove down from London. The altar, alcoves and pillars were decorated with flowers, and the churchyard path and lawn were covered with hundreds of wreaths and floral tributes.

'Pride of place were given to those sent from Buckingham Palace by the Queen, and Clarence House by the Queen Mother,' wrote the *Mid Sussex Times* of 22nd June 1979.

Barbara Cartland sent a wreath of vivid pink carnations with the words 'To Norman from his first customer, with loving memory of his kindness and the glamour he gave me over the years'.

The graves of Norman Hartnell, his sister Phyllis Stewart, her husband James Stewart, his mother Emma Mary Hartnell and his grandmother, Elizabeth Hartnell, are side by side under the shadow of an old yew tree.

His simple grey headstone describes him as 'a gentle knight . . . Dress designer to the Queens of England 1937–1979'.

There could be no finer or more fitting epitaph.

Fact File:

Clayton is at the foot of the Downs on the B2112, six miles north of Brighton.

Dame Grace working at the Heritage.

Dame Grace Kimmins
and Chailey Heritage School

'Wounded soldiers, fighting the battle for an independent life,' was Dame Grace Kimmins' description of disabled children and adults.

This outlook drove her to become a pioneer of education for children suffering from rickets, tuberculosis and malnutrition, eventually co-founding the Chailey Heritage Craft School and Hospital, formerly the Chailey Union Workhouse, with her life-long friend Alice Rennie.

Born in Lewes, East Sussex, on 6th May 1870, she was the daughter of taylor-draper James Hannam and his wife Thyrza Rogers. After school, she joined a Wesleyan mission in the east end of London where, as Sister Grace, she worked closely with poor and underprivileged families.

Their plight inspired her to found the Guild of Poor Things, a name she later altered to the Guild of Poor Brave Things. With Alice Rennie, she provided tea, play activities and readings for disabled adults and children in Cleveland Hall, West London, her first venue for Guild meetings. She was also influenced by the popular Victorian novelist Juliana Horatio Ewing's book *The Story of a Short Life*, and her quote: 'Laetus sorte mea' – 'Happy in my lot' which Grace adopted as her motto for the Guild.

At the time, society viewed children born with disabilities as useless and unable to contribute in a meaningful way. Consequently, they received no education, were malnourished and many were forced to fend for themselves with a begging bowl on the streets of London. Their future was grim until Grace, a small woman with a big heart and a big dream, determined to give the children a fair chance.

On 28th July 1898, at Southwark Park Wesleyan Chapel, packed with poor disabled children and their parents, Grace married Dr Charles Kimmins, a child psychologist and an inspector of schools for the London County Council (LCC). The couple lived in London, where their two young sons were subsequently born. The Kimmins provided education and welfare for poor disabled children through the Guilds. Grace also wrote *Polly of Parker's Rents* (1899), highlighting the lives of children living in slums.

In 1902 the Kimmins returned to the Sussex countryside, believing that fresh country air was more beneficial and therapeutic than London. Grace and Alice Rennie bought a run-down, rat-infested former workhouse without gas, electricity or a telephone at North Common, Chailey in East Sussex.

Grace had no medical training or educational qualifications, but this did not deter her. She set about building a school for disabled children where they could receive both medical care and, most importantly, a trade or craft. With her customary optimism, she instilled the children with a positive and cheerful outlook on life, with an emphasis on achievement without self-pity and where there was no such word as 'impossible'.

A year later, when the building was restored, Grace brought seven disabled boys – 'one for each day of the week' – down from the London slums to become the first residents. The boys assisted with improvements and the Chailey Heritage for Cripple Boys opened in 1903. (The term cripple was the norm at that time.) Her husband and philanthropists supported her, and with her unlimited enthusiasm, dedication and superb fund-raising skills, the school grew steadily.

In 1908 the Llangattock Heritage School for Cripple Girls was opened. Grace, wearing her white starched muslin cap and mauve frock, made sure that the girls were taught a craft to give them independence in adulthood, something that she saw as their heritage.

Her reputation grew and she lost no time in using her husband's contacts with the LCC to arrange for funding through rates for the children who came to Chailey. Boys learnt carpentry, which they put to good use making furniture for the school using local Sussex oak, and leather craft, a skill they used to make their own boots. Girls learnt cooking, needlework and housewifery skills and all children enjoyed games, gymnastics and music and movement.

A great believer in fresh air, Grace had the children, including babies from a few weeks, sleep outside all year round with a tarpaulin providing shelter from the elements and a ready supply of hot water bottles. The school had a no-nonsense Spartan approach, with doors and windows open in all weathers, something that Grace, addressed as the Commandant, insisted upon.

Each child made a wooden ladder to symbolise challenges in their lives that they would face and overcome. The children's first challenge was a writing test, beginning 'There's always room at the top'.

A great respecter of royalty, Dame Grace escorted many royal and aristocratic visitors around the Chailey workshops, and the children formed a line of honour to sing to them. Bishops and archdeacons preached at St Martin's Chapel under Grace's watchful eye, but if the sermon was too long she pressed a buzzer from the back of the church to alert the cleric to draw to a conclusion quickly!

The chapel is a well-known Sussex landmark, built of Sussex sandstone with a distinctive red-tiled roof. The spire is covered with oak shingles, at the suggestion of Rudyard Kipling, who took a keen interest in the school from its earliest days. The beautiful turquoise panelled ceiling is adorned with blue and gold leaf, with heraldic bosses and carved angels. Under the windows there are inscriptions to remember benefactors of the school and St Martin's Chapel.

Grace, once called in admiration 'the greatest beggar in England', was relentless in her imaginative fund-raising, with schemes such as the Golden Apple Appeal and through legacies and individual donations. She would launch completely unrelated but highly successful drives, such as the thanksgiving appeal when King George VI recovered from a bout of ill health.

Large donations poured in from eminent people in Britain and around the world, including members of the royal family, Robert Baden-Powell and Jesse Boot, the founder of Boots. The Duke of Norfolk was its president, and the Queen Mother and Princess Louise were patrons. The Queen Mother visited the school on six occasions, once in 1945 when she was accompanied by the young Princess Elizabeth (now Queen Elizabeth II) and her sister Princess Margaret Rose. On another occasion, the Queen Mother arrived in a red helicopter, much to the delight of the children. Another royal visitor was Princess Alice, Countess of Athlone, who restarted the sails of a restored windmill in front of large crowds who had gathered to watch the ceremony.

Locally, however, the reaction was very different when villagers on the Newick side of the chapel made it clear that they did not want Chailey Heritage School in their midst. With her forthright manner, Grace responded briskly. She

The chapel at Chailey Heritage.

would not 'give the time of day' to their opposition, something she underlined by commissioning the chapel clock with only three faces – the one on the east, facing Newick, left blank.

During the First World War Chailey's work expanded when over 500 wounded soldiers and sailors were offered orthopaedic and prosthetic rehabilitation and the opportunity to learn a trade, an achievement that further enhanced Chailey's reputation. With the wounded servicemen about to take over the boys' quarters, the boys set about constructing wooden huts for themselves, patriotically named the Kitchener Huts. Afterwards the boys were rewarded when Lord Kitchener himself presented them with their first union jack.

Psychological support was given to soldiers who had lost a limb or had one amputated. A boy with the same disability would be 'matched' with the soldier to show him how to cope with his new circumstances and, at the same time, become the best of friends.

In 1917 the St Nicholas Home for Raid-Shock Children was opened on Trafalgar Day. Grace provided children who had had a limb blown off or lost their home with somewhere to recover both physically and mentally. The home, dubbed the 'House of Smiles' by Lord Riddell, one of its supporters, treated 590 children – most pictured smiling and playing games – until its closure in 1920.

The school continued to grow and adapt to the children's needs, and in 1924, the marine annexe at Tidemills near Newhaven was founded. The atmosphere was relaxed and informal, giving boys the chance to enjoy exercising in the fresh bracing sea air.

Many years later, when the Second World War broke out, Grace (nearly 70 years old, but as tireless as ever), immediately started fund-raising so that she could provide a home for 'blitzed babies and toddlers'. Children suffering from bronchitis, pneumonia and stress, who had been rescued from their bombed homes and air-raid shelters, received treatment at the enlarged Princess Elizabeth Clinic, opened in 1942.

However, in 1946 the forthcoming creation of the National Health Service brought a wind of change to the Heritage and a new style of management. Grace wrote to the governors asking to be relieved of her duties, acknowledging that 'advancing years and certain physical disabilities now make it impossible to continue with the day by day administration'.

In 1948 Grace experienced great changes in her life. After 50 years of marriage, she not only lost her ever-supportive husband Charles, but also Chailey Heritage, which was absorbed into the National Health Service. Yet despite such major adjustments, she continued to devote her time to the welfare of the Heritage, where she lived until she died at the King Edward VII Memorial Hospital in Haywards Heath on 3rd March 1954.

For her selfless achievements, Grace was made a CBE in 1927. She was also made a Dame of the British Empire in 1950 and a Dame of Grace of the Order of St John of Jerusalem.

Chailey Heritage School is a registered charity relying on donations to raise money for building work and equipment. Dame Grace's legacy of helping her 'wounded soldiers' continues so many years later through the unique, ongoing work of Chailey Heritage School – something she would have approved of.

Fact File:

Chailey Heritage School, Haywards Heath Road, North Chailey, East Sussex, BN8 4EF. Tel: 01825 724444.

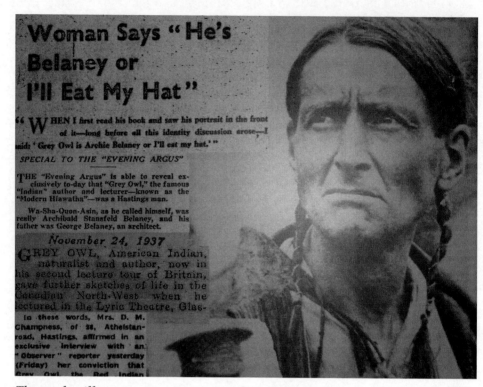

Woman Says "He's Belaney or I'll Eat My Hat"

" WHEN I first read his book and saw his portrait in the front of it—long before all this identity discussion arose—I said: 'Grey Owl is Archie Belaney or I'll eat my hat.' "

SPECIAL TO THE "EVENING ARGUS"

THE "Evening Argus" is able to reveal exclusively to-day that "Grey Owl," the famous "Indian" author and lecturer—known as the "Modern Hiawatha"—was a Hastings man.

Wa-Sha-Quon-Asin, as he called himself, was really Archibald Stansfeld Belaney, and his father was George Belaney, an architect.

November 24, 1937

GREY OWL, American Indian, naturalist and author, now in his second lecture tour of Britain, gave further sketches of life in the Canadian North-West when he lectured in the Lyric Theatre, Glas-

In these words, Mrs. D. M. Champness, of 24, Athelstan-road, Hastings, affirmed in an exclusive interview with an "Observer" reporter yesterday (Friday) her conviction that Grey Owl, the Red Indian

The truth will out: press reports revealing Grey Owl's true identity – By kind permission of Hastings Museum and Art Gallery.

'Grey Owl', Hastings
and the Little Princesses

'Grey Owl', known as the modern Hiawatha, was the world-famous North American Indian lecturer, broadcaster and writer of best-selling books on conservation and the Indian way of life.

But the reality was very different. He was in fact Archibald 'Archie' Stansfeld Belaney, born at 32 St James's Road, Hastings, Sussex on 18th September 1888. His father, George Furmage Belaney, was an alcoholic and spendthrift believed to have lived in America until his death in 1910. His mother, Kittie, was rumoured to have been only 13 years old when she married him.

Archie's father saw him no more than twice in his lifetime. To make matters worse, Kittie left her son in the care of his grandmother Julia and his strict but kind aunts Ada and Carrie. Archie was just two at the time. Very occasionally, he received a visit from his mother, accompanied by Hugh, Archie's brother who was later permanently institutionalised after the First World War.

From the age of eight to 11, Archie attended a small Anglican school, and he then attended Hastings Grammar School from 1899 to 1904. He was a tall and rebellious student, more like a red indian in his ways than an English schoolboy, but despite this eccentricity he excelled at English and French, for which he won a school prize.

At his home, 36 St Mary's Terrace, Hastings, he added excitement to his life by collecting animals and snakes which he kept in his menagerie in the attic. He read comics about the Wild West, played 'indians' and hooted like an owl with his friend and next-door neighbour George McCormick and his small group of friends in nearby St Helen's Woods. He also savoured every moment of Buffalo Bill's Wild West Show when it came to Hastings in 1903.

At the age of 16, he left school to work as a clerk in a lumberyard but hated it, wanting nothing more than to live in the Canadian wilderness with the indians. His aunts encouraged him, and on March 29th 1906 he boarded a ship bound for Canada, where he could live out his dreams.

Initially, he worked as a clerk in a Toronto department store before moving to Temagami, Northern Ontario, and then to Quebec, where he learnt how to trap and canoe and how to survive in the wilderness. He worked for some years as a trapper and met the Anishinaabe people of Tema-Augama, immersing himself in their language and customs.

On 23rd August 1910 he married Angele Egwuna, an Anishinaabe woman who taught him about her people. The marriage produced a child, but two years later, Archie, a womanizer who was fond of the bottle like his father before him, left his wife and child.

When the First World War broke out, he served in the 13th (Montreal) Battalion of the Black Watch in France from 1915. He still spoke with an English accent, but described himself as part Indian and was treated as such, something that pleased him. A loner, he used his shooting skills to become a sniper in France until he was wounded in the hand in January 1916 followed by a shrapnel wound to his foot on the 24th April.

When gangrene developed, he was treated in England at a number of infirmaries. During this time, whilst still married to Angele, he met and married his childhood sweetheart Ivy Holmes on 10th February 1917, but she divorced him in 1922 on the grounds of bigamy. In September 1917 he returned to Canada where, on November 30th, he received an honourable discharge and a full disability pension.

A spell as a forest ranger and wilderness guide followed, and by the 1920s he was signing himself 'Grey Owl'. As Grey Owl or 'Wa-sha-quon-asin' (meaning 'Great Horned Owl' or 'He-Who-Flies-By-Night'), he described

St Mary's Terrace, Hastings, where Archie Belaney lived as a lad.

himself as half-Indian. A great storyteller, he said he was born in Mexico in 1888. He claimed his blue eyes were inherited from his Scottish father and his swarthy complexion and rugged looks came from his Apache Indian mother, and that he had emigrated from the States to join the Ojibwa Indians in Ontario, Canada.

There were several short-lived relationships until 1925, when he married a Mohawk Iroquois woman, Gertrude Bernard, in an Indian ceremony. Anahareo as she became, was his most significant relationship. She was also the greatest influence in his adult life, persuading him to stop the cruelty of trapping in favour of writing about his life in the wilderness and the need to protect Canada's wildlife and forests.

His articles concerning the protection of beavers and the wilderness attracted the Dominion Parks Service, which employed him as a naturalist highlighting the need to protect Canada's forests and wildlife. His work and love of beavers spread, and in 1928 the National Parks Service made 'Beaver People', a film starring Grey Owl and Anahareo playing with their beaver cubs, Rawhide and Jellyroll.

He was appointed warden of Riding Mountain National Park, Manitoba, and in 1931 Grey Owl and Anahareo, accompanied by Rawhide and Jellyroll, moved into a small log cabin beside a picturesque lake in the park. However, due to unsuitable water conditions, they later moved to a 6m x 7m log cabin, Beaver Lodge, beside Ajawaan Lake in Prince Albert National Park – an environment more to the beavers' liking.

He worked for Prince Albert National Park from 1931 to 1938. The public's interest in Grey Owl's lifestyle grew, and he wrote many articles on the vanishing frontier, some for the English magazine *Country Life*, and four best-selling books under the name of Grey Owl, *Men of the Last Frontier* (1931), *Pilgrims of the Wild* (1934), *The Adventures of Sajo and her Beaver People* (1935) and *Tales of an Empty Cabin* (1936).

His popularity and confidence increased, and he undertook lectures supported by Anahareo. After lecturing in Montreal, he found himself described as a full-blooded Indian, something he saw as an advantage as it would make the audience more receptive to his message regarding wildlife and conservation. He never set the record straight, continuing to speak at parties, hotels and public halls, where he received generous collections.

In 1935, he embarked on his first strenuous lecturing tour of England. Tall and lanky, and dressed in Ojibwa costume with swarthy dyed skin, aquiline features and black braided hair tied back, he held his audiences spellbound – among them, at the London Palladium, the young David and Richard (later Lord) Attenborough.

However, when he spoke in Hastings at the White Rock Pavilion not far from his old playground, St Helen's Wood, his two aunts Ada and Carrie sat mesmerised in the audience. Amidst deafening applause, both recognised him but decided to keep his identity secret, preferring to read the numerous press reports describing their nephew taking England by storm and the royal family reading his books.

Two years later he returned to England for his second tour with a new wife, Anahareo having left him due to the strain of his tours and his writing commitments. On 10th December 1937, the highlight of his tour was a command performance at Buckingham Palace for Queen Mary, King George VI, Queen Elizabeth and the two young princesses Elizabeth and Margaret Rose.

Accompanied by his English publisher, Lovat Dickson, Grey Owl refused to perform unless there was a reversal of royal protocol. Instead of Grey Owl and Dickson sitting in the reception hall and standing when the royal family made their entrance in the usual way, on this occasion it would be the other way round!

Dickson described how Queen Mary, the royal family and Queen Elizabeth's parents, the Earl and Countess of Strathmore, sat good humouredly as Grey Owl, a showman down to his moccasins, made his grand entrance, saluting George VI with the words, 'How Kola', followed by a few token words in Ojibway meaning 'I come in peace, brother'.

Grey Owl spoke passionately about the Canadian forests and animals and about the plight of the North American Indians. The wide-eyed princesses hung on his words, and when Grey Owl's talk came to an end, the young Elizabeth pleaded, 'Oh, do go on!' The lecture and film show was such a success that Grey Owl gave the future Queen a ten-minute encore.

At the height of his success his luck ran out when Hastings resident Mary McCormick, the sister of his friend George McCormick who he had played with 30 years before, recognized him from the past. 'He's Belaney or I'll eat my hat', the *Evening Argus* reported on November 1937.

Fearing that his cover was about to be blown, and exhausted after months of touring Britain, the United States and Canada, he returned to Beaver Lodge at Ajawaan Lake. With his health at a low ebb, he was rushed to hospital, but three days later, on April 13th, 1938, he died of pneumonia aged 49. He was buried at Ajawaan Lake near Beaver Lodge, where his grave is marked with a soldier's cross recording two identities: 'A. Belaney' inscribed horizontally and 'Grey Owl', the name by which he was known throughout the world, displayed vertically.

After his death, glowing obituaries were replaced by exposures around the world denouncing him as a hoax, a fraud and the greatest literary impostor of all time. The disappointed public stopped buying his books and the conservation causes so dear to him suffered.

However, during the 1970s his books were re-discovered, and the scandal regarding his lack of Indian blood was replaced by a pride in his achievements as a conservation officer, lecturer, broadcaster and 'ambassador for the wild'.

Plaque at 36 St Mary's Terrace.

In Hastings he received posthumous recognition for his work. In 1988 the Grey Owl Society of Hastings celebrated the centenary of his birth by planting a Canadian Red Maple tree in the grounds of William Parker School, formerly Hastings Grammar School. His birthplace, 32 St James Road, has a plaque in his honour, and there is also a commemorative plaque in Hastings Country Park nature reserve.

Hastings Museum and Art Gallery has a permanent display dedicated to Grey Owl, with a replica of his log cabin. At 36 St Mary's Terrace, the home he shared with his grandmother and aunts, there is a further commemorative plaque (*above*), and in 1999 Lord Attenborough's film 'Grey Owl', starring Pierce Brosnan and Annie Galipeau, was shown for the first time.

An eloquent, larger than life figure considered by many to be the first conservationist long before the subject became popular, he gave a warning which, many years after his death, we cannot afford to forget: 'Remember, you belong to nature, not it to you.'

Fact File:

Hastings Museum and Art Gallery, Bohemia Road, Hastings, East Sussex, TN34 1ET. Tel: 01424 451052.
Hastings Country Park, 4 miles to the east of Hastings.

Patrick Hamilton's childhood home at 12, First Avenue, Hove.

Patrick Hamilton, 'The Charmer' and 'The West Pier'

Sussex writer Patrick Hamilton, the author of *Mr Stimpson and Mr Gorse* on which the television series 'The Charmer' starring Nigel Havers was based, was born at Dale House in Hassocks, Mid Sussex, on St Patrick's Day – 17th March – in 1904.

His father, Walter Bernard Hamilton (1863–1930), a non-practising barrister, and his second wife, Ellen Adele Day, née Hockley (1861–1934) were both minor novelists trapped by Edwardian middle class society in an unhappy marriage. Anthony Walter Patrick Hamilton was their third and last child. His early days were spent in a middle class home with servants and nannies to run the household, until his father's alcoholism and his inheritance squandered on drink and women left them in reduced circumstances.

From 1908 until the First World War, Patrick lived at 12 First Avenue, Hove, later commemorated by a plaque. During the war, the family lived in boarding houses in Chiswick and Hove, where Patrick became introverted and withdrawn. He was educated at Holland House School in Hove, Colet Court in Hammersmith and Westminster School until his mother removed him when he contracted Spanish Influenza. A London crammer marked the end of his formal education in 1919, when he was fifteen.

Disregarding his father's advice to train for a profession, he worked in a variety of low-paid jobs and as an actor under the stage name Patrick Henderson. In 1923 he became a full-time writer with the financial support of his mother Ellen, his sister Lalla and brother Bruce, and by the age of 19 he had completed his first novel, *Monday Morning*, published in 1925 by Constable, whose editor, the writer Michael Sadlier, became a great friend.

Run-down boarding houses, pubs and brothels in Brighton, Hove and London formed the backdrop for his novels, whose plots mirrored experiences in his own life – such as his obsession with a prostitute, depicted in his novel, *The Midnight Bell* (1929).

Small and slight, with horn-rimmed glasses, he secretly married Lois Marie Martin on 6th August 1930, shortly after his father's death. At the time he was drinking and smoking heavily, but Lois took over his finances and moderated his consumption of alcohol, enabling him to write *The Siege of Pleasure* in 1932.

In the 1930's, following his brother Bruce's visit to the Soviet Union, Hamilton was attracted to the works of Karl Marx and Lenin. His sympathy for the 'semi-proletariat' inspired a satirical attack on capitalism and the capitalist culture in his book *Impromptu in Moribundia* (1939).

Despite his heavy drinking, he took pride in his appearance, wearing elegant and fashionable clothes. However in 1932, at the height of his success, he was run over by a drunken driver whilst walking with his sister and wife in London. This left him with a withered left arm, a limp and disfiguring scars on his nose and forehead. He spent three months in hospital, endured plastic surgery and multiple operations and the emotional scars remained with him for the rest of his life. Once again he wrote about his personal experiences of his accident in *The Siege of Pleasure*.

Maimed and unfit for active service during the Second World War, he worked for the Entertainments National Service Association and served as a firewatcher during air raids, whilst continuing to write successfully. However, his personal life was fraught with difficulties, and in 1948 he began an extra-marital affair with Lady Ursula Stewart, née Chetwynd-Talbot, known to her friends as 'La'.

For many years Hamilton lived from Monday to Friday with La, an author who wrote under the pseudonym Laura Talbot, and at weekends with his wife Lois. Not surprisingly, the two women never became friends despite knowingly 'sharing' Hamilton. Hamilton divorced Lois in 1953 and married La the following year, but the triangular affair continued.

Drawing from his own experiences, Hamilton wrote sympathetically about lonely men and women and their solitary, melancholy lives in shabby hotels and dingy boarding houses. Many aspects of modern life he disliked, particularly

The wreck of the West Pier today.

the car – describing an England smothered in 'metal beetles' in his 1953 novel, *Mr Stimpson and Mr Gorse*.

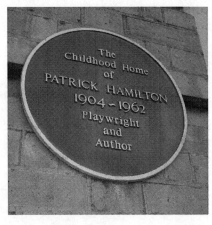

Personal setbacks and an ever growing addiction to drink failed to diminish his popularity on both sides of the Atlantic. His two most successful plays were *Rope* in 1929 (known as *Rope's End* in America and made into a film by Alfred Hitchcock in 1948), and *Gaslight* in 1938 (later filmed in America as 'Angel Street' in 1942).

The *Gorse Trilogy*, based on sexual predator and conman Ernest Ralph Gorse, comprised *The West Pier* (1952); *Mr Stimpson and Mr Gorse* (1953) and *Unknown Assailant* (1955), Hamilton's last published work.

With his unique style and acerbic wit, he was highly regarded in the literary world. J.B. Priestley wrote: 'He is the novelist of innocence, appallingly vulnerable, and of malevolence, coming out of some mysterious darkness of evil.' Graham Greene described *The West Pier* as 'the best novel ever written about Brighton'. John Betjeman also admired Hamilton's descriptions of inter-war London street culture combined with a distinctive Dickensian style of narrative and a conservative approach.

Recently, there has been a strong revival of interest in his work. In September 2005 BBC 2 screened an adaptation of his *Twenty Thousand Streets Under the Sky,* which was reshown on BBC 4 in January 2006. His most famous work, *Hangover Square: A Story of Darkest Earl's Court* (1941), continues to sell well today in paperback form.

The final years of Hamilton's life were unproductive blighted by drink, ill-health and a bout of depression. In desperation, La's former husband advised Hamilton to undergo electroshock therapy, but without success. La and his former wife Lois nursed him in his final years, until his death from cirrhosis of the liver and kidney failure on September 23rd 1962 at his home in Sheringham, Norfolk. He was just 58.

Fact File:

Patrick Hamilton's childhood home can be seen at 12, First Avenue, Hove. The West Pier, the subject of his 1952 novel, has since declined into wrack and ruin.

The village sign at Sedlescombe, where Patience Strong last settled in Sussex.

The Patience Strong Phenomenon, a One-Woman Industry

'I'm against that. It would fill Kent full of foreigners on motor-cycles.'

So said the world-famous poet Patience Strong when she heard about the building of the Channel Tunnel, a pet hate, in the Sixties. Often outspoken, with controversial opinions on religion, politics and the modern age, she is best remembered for her inspiring poetry and uplifting messages.

Born Winifred Emma May on 4th June 1907 in South London to Alfred and Nell May, she had an older sister, Connie, and a younger brother affectionately known as 'Boy'. Her childhood centred on Sunday school and, with her sister, visiting the public library. They enjoyed reading poetry and reciting poems to each other at night.

As a child she enjoyed family holidays in 'magic' Brighton, where she loved the thrill of the Palace Pier and West Pier, Brighton Pavilion and Volk's Railway trundling along the seafront. She also loved the Downs and going by bus to Rottingdean to see the house where her hero Rudyard Kipling had lived.

Her family were regular visitors to music halls, and from an early age she not only played the piano by ear, but composed verses and lyrics. She attended the local school in Catford, followed by Cusack's College, where she took a secretarial course which enabled her to obtain a post in a patent office.

Whilst working as a secretary she submitted her poems for publication, but it was not until 1922 that she had her first poem published in *Nash's Magazine* for one guinea. More success followed, and her poems appeared in *The Strand* and *Good Housekeeping*.

Her talent as a pianist led to a job in the Manor Mount Club in Forest Hill and a meeting with the composer Frederick Drummond, who was so impressed by her lyric 'To Sing Awhile' that he set it to music and Keith Prowse published it. She received three guineas for an outright sale but no royalties, something that did not bother her as she was only interested in expanding her writing opportunities.

After this the Manor Mount Club promptly offered her full-time employment and by the age of 21 she had more than a hundred published songs to her credit, the most famous being the well-known tango 'Jealousy', which was later recorded by Gracie Fields, Vera Lynn and Billy Fury.

Success did not go to her head, and she was equally happy writing advertising jingles for Ovaltine, furniture polish and face powder, which she described as 'a change from the moonlight-and-roses love songs'.

Above: The Street in Sedlescombe, Patience Strong's last home.

Below: The Sussex Downs where she loved to walk.

She continued writing songs, and in 1930 composed a lyric, *Princess Elizabeth*, to celebrate the fourth birthday of Princess Elizabeth, later Queen Elizabeth II. But shortly afterwards *Princess Elizabeth* was completely overshadowed by Lawrence Wright and Joe Gilbert's song *Amy wonderful Amy*, written to celebrate the solo flight to Australia of Amy Johnson, something that had never been achieved before.

Spurred on by her successes and inspired by Wilhelmina Stitch, a famous verse-writer for the *Daily Sketch*, she approached the editor of the *Daily Mirror* in 1935 with the suggestion that she write a daily poetry column for them. She made a good impression and was invited to return the next day with 18 more poems and a suitable pseudonym.

That evening the problem was solved when a friend visited her bearing a gift, a book by Adeline D.T. Whitney called *Patience Strong* – the perfect pseudonym. The next day, she reappeared with more poems and her new name and was promptly hired.

In 1931, she married Frederick Williams, an architect known affectionately as 'Paddy' or 'the black-haired Celt'. The couple had first met at a Welsh yachting regatta five years earlier, and for both it was love at first sight. In her autobiography she wrote: 'This stranger had stepped out of his boat into my life and I was to love him until he died thirty-nine years later.'

The marriage was childless but very happy, with shared interests including walking in the Sussex countryside and holidays in Britain and the Holy Land, which as devout Christians was particularly important to them.

In her personal life she experienced deep sorrow in 1935, when her beloved sister Connie died of cancer aged 29. Sustained by her Christian beliefs in life after death, Patience wrote that Connie, who was so gentle and special to her, 'came alive in a way that would never have been possible had she lived'. As a last farewell, she wrote 'Love Laughs At Death', which was interred with her sister's coffin.

During World War II, servicemen and their families were comforted by the many inspirational poems which she wrote in the small, cramped study of her home, conveniently situated next door to the post office. Often a crumpled, much-read Patience Strong poem was found in the wallets of men who had died in conflict. Her daily poems appeared in 'The Quiet Corner' of the *Daily Mirror* until 1946, when she moved to the *Sunday Pictorial*, later the *Sunday Mirror*, where her regular column appeared over several decades.

Conservative and old-fashioned in her outlook, she thoroughly disliked the effect of television, which she blamed for 'Thingery, the lust for Things, not because of their beauty or their usefulness, but because of their popularity'. She had no interest in food, money or fame, being at one point perfectly content to live in a small two-up, two-down cottage where she could work in peace.

In 1967, she married Guy Cushing, a retired buyer for a departmental store whom she had known many years earlier. During this time she wrote *The Other Side of the Coin,* and she was made a Freeman of the City of London in 1970. But despite her achievements, her happiness was marred by Guy's progressive ill-health and his subsequent death in 1979, after just 12 years of marriage.

She described herself as a one-woman industry, seeing no need for a secretary or a new typewriter. Instead, she continued typing all her work on a heavy, antiquated Royal until it finally gave up under the strain.

Dubbed the 'Patience Strong phenomenon' by her publishers, she wrote for numerous magazines, including *Woman's Own* for over 40 years and *This England* for 30 years. Two recordings of her poems were made, several anthologies were published and her work appeared in greetings cards and calendars throughout the world.

A lover of Sussex throughout her life, she lived in the county for many years, with homes in Winchelsea, Woodmans, near Battle, and finally The Street in Sedlescombe, East Sussex where she died in 1990 aged 83 at her home, Sunnyside.

Her book *Thoughts for Every Day* was reprinted in 2004, and her inspiring poems celebrating the countryside, the beauty of nature, Christianity and inner strength continue to be as popular as ever.

Fact File:

Sedlescombe is near Battle and St Leonards, East Sussex.

Rowland Emett,
'The Ditchling Tinkerer'

Rowland Emett who lived in picturesque Wild Goose Cottage in East End Lane, Ditchling, from 1954 until his death in 1990, is perhaps best remembered as the inventor of the flying car for the1967 film 'Chitty Chitty Bang Bang', produced for Caractacus Potts, played by Dick Van Dyke. Another of his Ditchling inventions was his Veteran Car of the Future, designed to run on nothing more than boiled after-shave lotion!

Born in New Southgate, London, on 22nd October 1906, Emett was the elder son of Arthur Emett, a businessman and occasional amateur inventor, and his wife, Alice, née Veale. Emett's birth certificate registered him as Frederick Roland but throughout his life, despite signing himself Rowland Emett, he was variously known as Roland/Rowland/Emmet/Emett.

The young Emett was educated at Waverley Grammar School, Birmingham where his teachers described him as 'lazy' in everything except art in which he

Wild Goose Cottage, Ditchling.

excelled. He amused himself caricaturing his masters and machinery of all descriptions. At the age of 11 he wrote publishable poems, and when he was 14 he took out a world patent for a pneumatic volume control for the acoustic gramophone.

For a brief period Emett studied art at Birmingham school of Arts and Crafts, during which time he painted Cornish Harbour, a landscape hung at the Royal Academy in 1931. For several years he obtained work in a commercial art studio, and, when work was hard to find during the depression, he continued drawing imaginary and outlandish cars for his own amusement.

In 1939 Emett submitted his drawings to *Punch,* only to be rejected by the art editor Kenneth Bird (alias Fougasse) with the words 'not quite . . . but very ingenious'. Emett persevered, and his second submission was accepted. He soon became one of the most popular cartoonists at *Punch,* eventually becoming the magazine's cartoon editor.

His cartoon of a train named Nellie, created for *Punch* in 1944, was a patriotic buffer which remained popular throughout the Fifties, appearing in *Nellie Come Home* and *A New World for Nellie.* Nellie and other well-known trains, Humphrey or Bard of Avon, generally appeared with gossamer-fine cross-hatching or in subtle washes on half-page drawings. The three most famous Emett steam engines were Nellie, Neptune and Wild Goose.

During the war, when Emett was occupied as a draughtsman for the Air Ministry, he continued perfecting his cartoon skills. On 12th April 1941 he married Mary Evans, the daughter of a Birmingham silversmith, and from then on the methodical Mary took over her husband's chaotic business affairs.

His popularity grew, and he moved on from *Punch* to *Life* magazine in America. He received $12,300 for a 12-page spread in *Life* (5th July, 1954), enabling him to buy Wild Goose Cottage, where he lived with his wife Mary and their daughter Claire. In 1963 he was featured in a British Pathe newsreel building a sculpture from junk in his studio behind his Ditchling home, named after his favourite train. Also featured were his assistant, Denis Newman, his 16-year-old daughter, Claire, seen in the garden painting one of her father's models, and strange automatons attached to a large moving umbrella structure.

Multi-talented as a cartoonist and engineer, Emett's 'Gothic-Kinetic' sculptures frequently consisted of coal scullies, lampshades, spoons, bellows and assorted junk. Emmet said of his Things constructed at his workshop at The Old Forge in Streat: 'My machines are friendly, they are happy, they crave love, and I really think they get it.'

Comparisons were sometimes made with the drawings of William Heath Robinson and Rube Goldberg, but these rarely became functioning devices, whereas Emett's cartoons often became working models.

Artist Louise Gardner's impression of Rowland Emett's Jubilee bear in his 'bearoplane'

In 1951, at the Festival of Britain, he built his first amazing machine, a 15inch-gauge real-life version of the Far Tottering & Oyster Creek Railway complete with the first three-dimensional Emett steam engines, Nellie, Neptune and Wild Goose, the flying engine.

It was such a success that other machines with humorous names were built over the next thirty years, his many admirers including royalty, statesmen, politicians and the general public of all ages. The Exploratory Moon-probe Lunacycle 'Maud' and 'SS Pussiwillow II' were exhibited at Washington's National Museum of Air and Space. Other Emett working creations are shown every December at the Ontario Science Centre.

In 1944 Emett illustrated *Anthony & Antimacassar*, a children's book about a china pig and a railway train written by his wife Mary. He continued illustrating, his work ranging from illustrations of books by Walter de la Mare to advertisements for Guinness.

Fair haired and fresh-faced, he carried his years lightly, bearing a striking resemblance to the late Danny Kaye, the actor and comedian. In 1978 he was awarded an OBE for his 'services to art and science' yet, despite his global fame, he remained a shy, mild-mannered Englishman and a master of British eccentricity. Of his outlandish machines, Emett said affectionately: 'They are doing a little job for England. You see, they spread the idea of madness.'

In Ditchling Emett contributed to the design of St Margaret's Church of England primary school, attending many school plays with his wife Mary. In 1983 he invented Ditchling's Jubilee bear in his 'bearoplane' and he was a judge at the Teddy Bear Fair.

On 13th November 1990, aged 84, Rowland Emett died in a Hassocks nursing home. The *Mid Sussex Times* of 20th November 1990 wrote in his obituary that, at Christmas time, 'his corner of the village had its own special decoration – the Teddy Bear Father Christmas suspended in his unique flying machine'.

In November 2003 MGM released a 'Chitty Chitty Bang Bang' special edition, including a ten-minute feature of 'The Ditchling Tinkerer', showing Emett developing his wacky inventions for the film.

So many years later, his memory and his 'Things' continue to amuse and fascinate the world as much as ever.

Fact File:

Ditchling is under Ditchling Beacon and north of Brighton.

Jack and Jill Windmills, Henry Longhurst and the Film Industry

Perched on the top of the South Downs above the hamlet of Clayton are two familiar sights – the husband and wife pair of windmills known as Jack and Jill Windmills.

With a commanding view of the area, privately owned Jack is a black, brick tower mill built in 1866, whilst Jill, owned by Mid Sussex District Council, is a white post mill built in 1821. Originally Jill resided on the outskirts of Brighton under the name of 'Lashmar's New Mill'. However, in 1852, when the land she stood on was required for redevelopment, she was moved in sections and hauled by teams of oxen to her present home beside Jack.

Since January 1979, much work has been done through The Jack and Jill Windmills Society for the preservation of Jill Mill, a registered charity. Today she has been fully restored to working order by the society's team of dedicated volunteers who meet every Saturday to carry out maintenance and keep her in good repair.

Jack (in the background) and Jill windmills at Clayton.

In the Twenties, the windmills were very popular with 'trippers' taking the train from London to Brighton and it is likely that they affectionately first coined the names Jack and Jill which have been used ever since.

On a clear evening these two landmarks can be seen for miles around, cutting a dramatic figure silhouetted against the night sky. Therefore it is not surprising that, in the summer of 1973, the film company Universal Pictures chose Jack, standing over 44ft from the ground, for the purpose of making a film 'The Black Windmill'.

Featuring a star-studded cast, including Michael Caine, Janet Suzman, Donald Pleasance, Dennis Quilley and Joss Ackland, the film – about a British agent's son who is kidnapped and held for a ransom of diamonds – had found the perfect setting.

Filming took six weeks. However, before the cameras could roll, the director, Don Siegel, felt that some restoration was required. New sweeps (sails) were fitted at a cost of £3,000 and the exterior of the mill was re-painted, while the underground tunnel leading from the granary to Jack got special treatment. It was generously doused with a special chemical, and during the scene when a gun was fired, the whole tunnel burst dramatically into flames right on cue!

Every bit as exciting as the film itself was the owner of the windmills, Henry Longhurst. Golfer, writer, broadcaster and raconteur, Henry Longhurst bought as he put it 'two derelict windmills and a nine-room wooden bungalow' where he and his family lived from 1953 to 1978. Not only was he a master golfer, but for over 45 years he was a regular contributor to the *Sunday Times*, writing

The Downs near Jack and Jill windmills.

more than a thousand articles without missing a Sunday – an achievement he was particularly proud of.

With his knowing wink, long silences and affable wit, he could not be ignored. When not attending golf tournaments in the many countries he visited, Henry could be seen driving up to the windmills in his trademark large, blue motor car to enjoy the quiet and tranquillity of the Sussex Downs, accompanied by his faithful bull terrier, Kerry.

A small, portly man – possibly broadened by his love of golf club bars around the world – Henry travelled to more than thirty countries on every continent. No mean golfer himself, he won a golf blue at Cambridge University and the German Amateur title in 1936, yet he always wrote about the sport in a light-hearted way, never taking the game too seriously. 'They say "practice makes perfect". Of course it doesn't. For the vast majority of golfers it merely consolidates imperfection,' he quipped.

Popular both in Britain and America, he was a man of many talents. He helped construct golf courses in such far-flung places as the Alps and the Persian Desert, wrote twelve light-hearted books and numerous articles on a variety of subjects, all peppered with his dry wit and keen observations of the human spirit. Wherever he was, the countryman in him ensured a great appreciation of not only golfing but the local trees, flowers and birds, both abroad and at his home on the South Downs with its profusion of snowdrops, daffodils and cowslips. He particularly enjoyed the stunning views of the Sussex Weald from the windmills as he recalled in his autobiography, first published in 1971, *My Life and Soft Times*:

> 'From the pier we look over to the Devil's Punchbowl at Hindhead,
> forty odd miles away; then across the Weald to the North Downs, and
> away on the right to the wireless masts of Crowborough – a
> stupendous, ever changing scene – and at night the distant lights
> of Burgess Hill's main thoroughfare look exactly as though we
> are approaching the runway.'

But the windmill's exposed position meant high winds. In 1987 the Great Storm swept across the south of England, battering the windmills with dire results. Wind speeds of 120 mph caused Jill's sweeps to turn against the brake, and the friction between the brake shoes and the brake wheel produced sparks which set Jill alight. Luckily all was not lost. Dedicated members of the Jack and Jill Windmills Society rushed to the blazing mill, where they successfully put the fire out. The storm damage took over 700 man-hours of voluntary labour to return the building to its original state.

The windmills have a fascinating and varied past. When Henry Longhurst and his family moved in, they quickly realised they weren't the only occupants. A ghostly presence, possibly a Mrs Anson, a previous owner who died of a chest complaint, could be heard coughing from 'Mrs Anson's room' in Jack Mill. As if that wasn't enough, old-fashioned servants' bells would ring loudly when, according to Henry 'there was not a soul in the place'.

Henry and his wife Claudine lived happily together at Clayton Windmills until his death on 21st July 1978. Henry gave Jill Mill into public ownership, and in July 1986 the official opening took place when his widow unveiled a plaque commemorating the occasion.

Today Jill is open on most Sundays between May and September from 2pm to 5pm. Admission is free. Learn about the intact skeleton of an Anglo-Saxon man unearthed beside Jack, and the war work carried out in the granary in 1915, when men and women toiled in dim light constructing fragile tail parts for World War I aircraft. View the miller's meticulous accounts, the spout room where milling takes place and, if weather conditions are suitable, enjoy Jill's majestic sweeps turning in the wind.

Fact File:

Jack and Jill Windmills are near Clayton Village, West Sussex.

Sussex Healer, Spiritualist and Psychic Betty Shine

Betty Shine, the healer, spiritualist and psychic, was a familiar figure to many people in Sussex where she lived and worked for many years.

She was born in Kennington in 1929 and evacuated during the war as a child. She then lived in Surrey and Spain before moving to Sussex, where her homes included a small cottage with views towards the Downs in Streat, and Westmeston, Ditchling and Silverdale in Hassocks.

Well known for her work healing people, her best-selling books, healing tapes and radio and television appearances, Betty was considered one of the most famous and influential mediums of the day. Her reputation as a clairvoyant and highly developed psychic with the ability to diagnose medical problems spread around the world, resulting in her receiving a thousand letters a week in her Hassocks mailbox – all of which she answered personally!

Betty Shine's home in Streat from 1990–91.

When she was growing up, Betty's gifts had not been easy for her to cope with. From the age of two she could hear voices and see shadowy figures, at that time an unwanted gift she inherited from her grandmother. She did not want to be a medium at all, describing mediumship as 'a mystery' which caused her much conflict and turmoil.

At the age of 20 Betty married and started a family. However, she always loved music and, while still in her 20s, she trained to be a professional opera singer. With her strong, clear voice like her idol Maria Callas, she performed in a variety of operatic roles including 'Queen of the Night' by Mozart. Music was a big part of her life, ranging from pop music to the lyrics played by pianist Russ Conway, but her all-time favourite was Frank Sinatra with 'I did It My Way', a song that she found inspirational.

Apart from music, Betty had always been interested in health and the healing aspects of mediumship, and it was this interest that made her decide to use her mediumship abilities to pass on messages from the spirit world for the benefit of others. All her life Betty had blocked out the voices until, at the age of 45, she finally used her abilities as a medium for the first time. In her book *My Life As A Medium* she described how her friend's late mother had asked her to pass on a message to her daughter who exclaimed: 'I didn't know you were a medium', to which Betty replied: 'Neither did I!'

Every day was packed with appointments – healing through the laying-on-of-hands, colour-healing therapy and vitamin and mineral therapy. She also believed passionately in having a positive mental attitude, an approach that helped her cope with the challenges she faced, such as losing friends and suffering ridicule because many people thought mediums were frauds. But Betty was a free spirit with a strong character, and her belief in her powers helped her overcome intolerance to mediums and healers.

Betty believed very strongly in the power of mind energy, something that showed itself when she appeared at 11 o'clock at night on 'The Eleventh Hour' presented by Peter Quinn on Southern Sound, the radio station in Portslade. Betty was talking about mind control and the power of the mind when the console and all the controls started flashing. The whole building blacked out, the air-conditioning also packed in and the heat in the studio started building up rapidly.

After the interview, it transpired that the station's electricity supply had blown, and two out of three emergency generators were out of action, but the studio that Betty was broadcasting in was the only one left with power. She put this down to the fact that she was spreading the word and the power of mind magic, which she wrote about in her book of the same name. *Mind Magic*, which explains how mediums receive messages, the Universal Mind and how absent healing is given, subsequently became a *Sunday Times* bestseller.

A multi-talented person, her powers as a clairvoyant were so accurate that Betty foresaw the 11th September 2001 tragedy, drawing planes colliding in the air, smoke, bodies and two towers – the Twin Towers – collapsing. Bewildered, she did not understand what she was 'seeing' until it appeared on television afterwards.

Her health had caused her many worries but once she began using her powerful gifts as a medium and healer, it started to improve. However, when she was only 59 it was confirmed that Betty had a life-threatening heart defect needing open-heart surgery, which she bravely submitted to. Five months after the first operation and months of unexplained pain, a second operation was performed, as all the titanium wire used to join the sternum had corroded. This is very unusual, as titanium is considered practically corrosion resistant. But Betty's healing powers and the strong electrical energy that ran through her had corroded them – something that made perfect sense to Betty!

Her health improved, enabling her to focus her attention on writing books. These became best-sellers, and in the decade before her death she wrote eleven books detailing many near-death experiences, astral travel and evidence of survival after death – 'survival evidence'.

Sadly, more health problems dogged her, and the last eighteen months of Betty's life were fraught with difficulties. But, despite her failing health, Betty maintained her belief that it was better to give than to receive, writing many uplifting poems on scraps of paper and the back of envelopes whenever she was inspired.

After Betty's death of heart failure on 26th March 2002, 101 of her poems appeared in *Shine On – Visions of Life,* collated by her daughter Janet Shine as a tribute to her mother's strength and courage.

Betty lived her life 'her way' like her idol Frank Sinatra. She gave great happiness and support to so many people around the world, and today her memory and the work she did with her daughter Janet Shine live on as strong as ever.

Fact File:

Silverdale is between Hassocks and Ditchling.

Royal Crescent, Brighton. Lord Olivier lived at no. 4.

Laurence Olivier, Kippers and the Brighton Belle

On 29th June 1934 Margaret Hardy, the mayor of Brighton, launched a new luxury Pullman train service on the Southern Railway between London and Brighton. It had originally been named the Southern Belle, and Councillor Hardy, flanked by two officials and two railway guards, now officially renamed the Pullman electric train the Brighton Belle – a train offering luxury rail travel for commuters travelling the 53 miles between Brighton and London.

The renaming occurred following the electrification of Southern Railway's London-Brighton railway line in 1933, when three modified five car Pullman multiple unit trains designated 5BEL replaced the steam hauled Southern Belle service and the Brighton Belle was born.

The British Pullman is named after an American, George Mortimer Pullman, who described Pullman carriages as 'palaces on wheels', an apt description for the rich and famous lucky enough to travel surrounded by the splendours of the Brighton Belle.

Carriages in the first class section of the Belle were given names typical of the Thirties: Gwen, Mona, Doris, Hazel, Audrey and Vera. A stove warmed passengers during cold British winters; there were Edwardian style toilet and washroom facilities to have a wash and brush-up; and uniformed Pullman staff provided tea and freshly prepared sandwiches. Plush upholstery, table lamps with soft pink lampshades, highly polished brass fittings and the sumptuous Pullman umber and cream décor made it an unforgettable trip.

When the Second World War broke out, Audrey and Vera were damaged in an air raid on Victoria Station in 1940. Both were repaired, and years later Audrey served the royal family when she carried the Queen, the Queen Mother and Prince Philip to review the Fleet in 1953, while others were involved in national events when only a Pullman carriage would do.

To avoid further war damage the trains' titles and destination roof boards were removed, and the Belle was taken out of service. However, Belle services complete with wartime rations and war-weary train staff returned for duty until another bombing attack in May 1942 forced them into storage until October 1947, when the Brighton Belle was reinstated.

In 1948, the Belle was nationalised and became part of British Railways. The carriages were given a face-lift in 1955, but the ride was less than smooth and they failed to meet BR's more modern standards. Nevertheless, the Belle

The Walk of Fame plaque.

remained popular, particularly with the many actors and actresses who lived in Brighton. It gave them an opportunity to read their lines in a relaxed atmosphere and provided a non-stop service lasting approximately an hour. It was also regular, punctual and ideal for late night performances.

One of the greatest actors of modern times, Laurence Olivier, who lived at 4 Royal Crescent, Brighton was one of the regular passengers who travelled on the Brighton Belle. He was mortified when he learned that the morning service Brighton Belle express train to London had withdrawn one of his favourite refreshments from the menu – grilled kippers at breakfast! With the support of the local press, he immediately launched a battle to save them: the kippers remained but the train itself was axed only months later.

Sadly, the unique Brighton Belle electric Pullman train was expensive to run and, with the passage of time, decidedly wobbly on its wheels. The Belle and her white-jacketed waiters, deep carpets and plush upholstery was out of step with BR's policy of standardising train services, and so her days were numbered.

In 1967, BR repainted and refurbished the trademark umber and cream décor of the Pullman cars with their own much less attractive colours - blue and grey. In addition to this, BR disapproved of names for trains, and those such as the Newhaven Continental Express, the Eastbourne Pullman service and the Bournemouth Belle disappeared.

Other casualties were the withdrawal of Pullman carriages. However, the name 'Brighton Belle' continued for a little while longer but with the logo of British Railway instead of the more impressive Pullman badge – much to the annoyance of faithful Belle devotees.

The Brighton Belle outlived all the other Belle Pullman services, continuing until 30th April 1972 when she ran for the last time. 'Champagne' and 'cheese and wine' specials were sold out to faithful passengers determined to travel in style just once more. However, on 1st May 1972 the service was withdrawn and, with it, there came the end of an era.

After the closure many of the original carriages were incorporated in the equally glamorous Venice Simplon-Orient Express, and the other Pullman cars were snapped up. Some were used as restaurants, while others were bought by railway museums such as the volunteer-run Bluebell Railway Line between Horsted Keynes and Sheffield Park, thus preserving their unique qualities.

The Brighton Belle has not been forgotten. On 14th January 2003 an inauguration ceremony complete with a jazz band was organised at Brighton station, attended by famous Brighton residents Anna Wing, Carol Kaye, Chris Eubank, Leo Sayer and Dora Bryan, a former regular Belle commuter. The Venice Simplon-Orient Express loaned two superbly restored carriages, Vera and Audrey, and the Brighton Walk of Fame commemorated the event with a plaque on the Brighton station concourse.

Many years later, there are plans to bring back the Brighton Belle once more. Leading the campaign to revive the London to Brighton service in time for the 2012 London Olympics is Denis Dunstone, a railway enthusiast of the 5Bel Trust. In February 2009 the Trust began working hard to raise £500,000 to put together a five-car train fitted with new electrical equipment and restore the carriages to their original splendour.

Lord Olivier would be delighted. Roll on the Brighton Belle!

Fact File:

The Bluebell Railway's main station is at Sheffield Park, East Sussex. Horsted Keynes railway station is just outside the village, 5 miles north east of Haywards Heath.

Acknowledgements

I would like to thank the following for all their help and encouragement: My husband Rupert for accompanying me on my treks throughout Sussex, the Brighton History Centre, Connie Booth, Barry and Charmian Deller, Adrian Gardner, Louise Gardner, Sarah Warner, Haywards Heath Library and Roger Booth, editor of *South Downs Living* for permission to reprint articles which I wrote for *SDL*. I would also like to thank David Arscott at Pomegranate Press for his support and guidance in the making of this book.

Sources, picture credits and other acknowledgements

The Legend and History of Devil's Dyke:
Mr Nick Blackett of the National Trust at Devil's Dyke.
Ernest Ryman: *Devil's Dyke In Old Picture Postcards* and *The Devil's Dyke, A Guide*
The Devil's Dyke Times
The National Trust
Ted Power – *Brighton and Sussex* http://www.btinternet.com/~ted.power/d005.html
Wikipedia, the free encyclopaedia – Devil's Dyke, Sussex

'Mad Jack' Fuller of Brightling and his follies
J.P.J. Entract: *Oxford Dictionary of National biography* – Fuller, John (1757–1834), politician and eccentric
Geoff Hutchinson: *Fuller, the life and times of John Fuller of Brightling 1757– 1834*
Wikipedia, the free encyclopaedia: http://en.wikipedia.org/wiki/John'Mad Jack' Fuller – John 'Mad Jack'

William Borrer, famous 19th century botanist of Henfield
Henfield Library: *William Borrer, Botanist* by Maude Robinson; *Sussex County Magazine*, Vol. XIII, January to December 1939; *Ed.* Arthur Beckett
Henfield Museum
Henfield Parish Council
Dr T.A Cope, Herbarium, Royal Botanic Gardens, Kew
P.E. Kell: *Oxford Dictionary of National Biography (DNB)* – Borrer, William (1781–1862), botanist

The Sussex Love Story of Charles Stewart Parnell and 'Kitty' O'Shea
O'Shea, Katharine (K.W. Parnell): *Charles Stewart Parnell* (Cassell, 1914)
Frank Callanen: *Oxford DNB*: Parnell, (née Wood; other married name O'Shea)
    Katharine (1845–1921)
Val Brown: http://www.womenofbrighton.co.uk/katieoshea.htm "Kitty" O'Shea –
    Katharine Parnell 1845–1921
Steyning Museum and Worthing Library

Blood, Sweat and Tears on the Balcombe Viaduct
Roland Lewis: *What the Victorians did for Sussex* (Snake River Press)
http://www.historylearningsite.co.uk/navvies.htm
Engineering Timelines: Ouse Viaduct, Balcombe
Muriel V. Searle : *Down the line to Brighton*
Rupert Taylor: 'Flight of Fancy' – *South Downs Living*, June 2009

Bishop James Hannington, Sussex Martyr of Hurstpierpoint
The Rev'd John Joyce, Rector of Hurstpierpoint
The late Bishop James Hannington: *Peril and Adventure in Central Africa*
    (published posthumously)
E.C. Dawson: J*ames Hannington, A history of his life and work 1847–1885*
E. Jackson: *The First Forty Years* – Bishop Hannington Memorial Church, Hove

School Founder Canon Nathaniel Woodard of Henfield
Ardingly, Hurstpierpoint and Lancing Colleges
Janet Pennington: *Oxford DNB* – Woodard, Nathaniel (1811–1891)
Henfield Museum
Peter King: *Hurstpierpoint College 1849–1945*
Jeremy Tomlinson: *Lancing College, A Portrait*

'Dr Brighton' and Wounded Indian Soldiers of the Great War
Indian soldiers at the Royal Pavilion. By kind permission of www.black-history.org.uk
Brighton History Centre, Brighton Museum and Art Gallery – Newspaper cuttings
    of the *Brighton Gazette* and the *Argus*
http://www.black-history.org.uk/ -Brighton and Hove Black History
Joyce Collins – *Dr Brighton's Indian Patients December 1914–January 1916*
Bert Williams: http://www.mybrightonandhove.org.uk – Military Hospitals: The
    First World War

The White Dome of the Chattri, Memorial to Our Indian Comrades
Mr Davinder Dhillon, Organiser of the annual Chattri Memorial Service
Brighton History Centre: *Brighton Herald*, Saturday, February 5, 1921;
    Sussex Daily News 2 Feb.1921
Brighton and Hove Black History: *The Chattri Memorial*
www.chattri.com: The Chattri Memorial Service
Exhibition at Sussex University
www.black-history.org.uk

Danny, Lloyd George and the Armistice Talks
Mr Richard Burrows, owner of Danny, and Mr Ivar Graham, archivist and resident of Danny
Kenneth Jolly: *Sussex Life*, June 1965 – 'Danny, The Story of a Country House'.
Country Houses Association: Danny, Hurstpierpoint, Sussex
Evening Argus, 22 February 1974
Ian Ivatt: *Journal of Liberal History*, Issue 46, Spring 2005 – 'Frances Stevenson, Lloyd George and the Surrey – Sussex Dimension
www.dannyhouse.org.uk/history.html: The History of Danny
A J P Taylor *Ed.*: *My Darling Pussy*
War diary of Sir George Riddell

The Brighton Pylons, the Duke and Duchess of York and Sir Herbert Carden
Wikipedia: List of Landmarks and Notable Buildings of Brighton and Hove
Evening Argus, December 28th 1973: When Brighton burst its bounds
My Brighton and Hove
Brighton History Centre: *Sussex Daily News*, Thursday, 31st May 1928

G.K. Chesterton, Ditchling and Father Brown
*John L. Allen Jr.: *National Catholic Reporter*, V. 6, No.3, Sept. 15, 2006
American Chesterton Society: www.chesterton.org
Janet Cragg: Ditchling Museum, Church Lane, Ditchling
Michael Ffinch: *K. Chesterton – A biography*
Priscilla Johnston: *Edward Johnston – A biography*
Dick Morley: *No Ordinary Place* (The Ditchling Society, May 2003)
Steve Porter: Chestertons, 1 The High Street, Ditchling

Rudyard Kipling, Literary Giant of Sussex
Many thanks to the Grange Museum and Art Gallery, Rottingdean, for permission to photograph the exhibits.
The National Trust, Bateman's, Burwash, East Sussex
David Arscott: *A Sussex Kipling, an anthology of poetry and prose*
Tonie & Valmai Holt: *My Boy Jack*
Rudyard Kipling: *Something of Myself*
Richard Knowles: *Sussex in Fiction*
Adam Nicolson: *The National Trust, Bateman's*
Michael Smith: http://www.kipling.org.ukrgSussex – Kipling's Sussex 2 & 3

Hassocks Inventor Magnus Volk and his Electric Railway
Mr Stuart Strong, Manager of Volk's Electric Railway, Brighton
Jenny Pulling: V*olk's Railway Brighton 1883–1983 Centenary*
Volk'srailway@brighton-hove.gov.uk
Alan A. Jackson: *Volk's Railway Brighton*
Conrad Volk: *Magnus Volk of Brighton*

John Logie Baird, Television Pioneer of Hastings

Many thanks to Hastings Museum and Art Gallery for granting permission to
    photograph the exhibits.
R.W Burns: *DNB* – Baird, John Logie (1888–1946), television engineer
Anthony Kamm and Malcolm Baird: *John Logie Baird, A Life*
http://www.1066.net/baird/ John Logie Baird in Hastings
Hastings Museum and Art Gallery: The John Logie Baird Exhibition

National Velvet and Enid Bagnold of Rottingdean

The Grange Museum and Art Gallery, Rottingdean
Richard Knowles: *Sussex In Fiction*
Nigel Nicolson: *DNB* article – Bagnold, Enid Algerine
Anne Sebba: *Enid Bagnold, The Authorised Biography*
Helena Wojtczak: *Notable Sussex Women – 580 biographical sketches*

Norman Hartnell; By Royal Appointment

Norman Hartnell's 1955 autobiography *Silver and Gold*
Norman Hartnell, Royal Pavilion Art Gallery and Museums, 1985
Sophie Jepson, English Heritage Corporate Communications
The Evening Argus, Monday, June 11, 1979
Mid Sussex Times – June 15th 1979 and June 22nd 1979
Edward Rayne, rev. Amy de la Haye: *DNB* – Hartnell, Sir Norman Bishop

Dame Grace Kimmins and Chailey Heritage School

With special thanks to Mrs Verena Hanbury, president of Chailey Heritage School
    for allowing me to photograph the young Grace Kimmins in the
Chailey Heritage Archives
David Arscott: *Chailey Heritage, A Hundred Years*
Verena Hanbury: 'Chailey Heritage School, Our History'
Seth Koven: *DNB* – Kimmins (née Hannam), Dame GraceThyrza (1870 –1954)
Ann Kramer: *Sussex Women*
Helena Wojtczak: *Notable Sussex Women – 580 biographical sketches*

'Grey Owl', Hastings and the little Princesses

Many thanks to Hastings Museum and Art Gallery for granting permission to
    photograph the exhibits.
Anahareo: *Grey Owl and I, A New Autobiography*
Lovat Dickson: *Wilderness Man, The Strange Story of Grey Owl*
Donald B Smith: *ONB* – Belaney, Archibald Stansfeld (called Grey Owl)
    1888–1938, imposter and conservationist
Wikipedia, the free encyclopaedia – Grey Owl
Wa-Sha-Quon-Asin (Grey Owl) – *Pilgrims of the Wild*

Patrick Hamilton, *The Charmer* and *The West Pier*
Natalie Blondel: *DNB* – Hamilton, (Anthony Walter) Patrick (1904–1962)
Harry Ransom Center, University of Texas, St Austin – Patrick Hamilton Collection
Wikipedia, the free encyclopaedia – Patrick Hamilton (dramatist)

The Patience Strong Phenomenon, a One-Woman Industry
The Daily Telegraph, August 31, 1990 – Patience Strong Obituary
Patience Strong: *With a Poem in my Pocket* (Autobiography)
Doreen Montgomery: *DNB* – Cushing (née May; other married name Williams),
    Winifred Emma (Pseud. Patience Strong) (1907–1990), author and poet
Wikipedia – Patience Strong

Rowland Emett, 'The Ditchling Tinkerer'
Ditchling Museum & Stoneywish Park, Ditchling
Richard Dalby: *The comic Illustrations of Rowland Emett*
Mid Sussex Times, 20 November, 1990
The Times, 16 November 1990
John Jensen: *DNB* – Emett, (Frederick) Rowland (1906–1990)

Jack and Jill Windmills, Henry Longhurst and the Film Industry
Mr Simon Potter of Jack and Jill Windmills Society for the Preservation of Jill Mill
Alistair Cooke: 'Letter from America' – In Memory of Henry Longhurst
Henry Longhurst: *My Life and Soft Times*
Simon Potter: *Clayton Windmills*
M. Wilson and K.Bowden: *The Best of Henry Longhurst*
www.allaboutsussex.co.uk

Sussex Healer, Spiritualist and Psychic Betty Shine
Wikipedia, the free encyclopedia – Betty Shine
Betty Shine: *My Life As A Medium*
Betty Shine: *Shine On – Visions of Life*

Laurence Olivier, Kippers and the Brighton Belle
Michael H.C. Baker: *London to Brighton, 150 years of Britain's premier holiday line*
http://www.brightonbell.com/index.php –The Brighton Belle Trust
Martin Pring & Andries Grabowsky: *Shamrock Trains*
http://shamrocktrains.com/railwaystories.html
Wikipedia, the free encyclopedia – Brighton Belle

Index